How to Survive Middle School

Zondervan/Youth Specialties Books

Adventure Games
Amazing Tension Getters
ArtSource™ Volume 1—Fantastic Activities
ArtSource™ Volume 2—Borders, Symbols, Holidays, and Attention Getters
Attention Grabbers for 4th-6th Graders (Get 'em Growing)
Called to Care
The Complete Student Missions Handbook
Creative Socials and Special Events
Divorce Recovery for Teenagers
Feeding Your Forgotten Soul (Spiritual Growth for Youth Workers)
Get 'em Talking
Good Clean Fun
Good Clean Fun, Volume 2
Great Games for 4th-6th Graders (Get 'em Growing)
Great Ideas for Small Youth Groups
Greatest Skits on Earth
Greatest Skits on Earth, Volume 2
Growing Up in America
High School Ministry
High School TalkSheets
Holiday Ideas for Youth Groups (Revised Edition)
Hot Talks
How to Survive Middle School (Get 'em Growing)
Ideas for Social Action
Incredible Stories (Get 'em Growing)
Intensive Care: Helping Teenagers in Crisis
Junior High Game Nights
Junior High Ministry
Junior High TalkSheets
The Ministry of Nurture
On-Site: 40 On-Location Programs for Youth Groups
Option Plays
Organizing Your Youth Ministry
Play It! Great Games for Groups
Quick and Easy Activities for 4th-6th Graders (Get 'em Growing)
Super Sketches for Youth Ministry
Teaching the Bible Creatively
Teaching the Truth about Sex
Tension Getters
Tension Getters II
Unsung Heroes: How to Recruit and Train Volunteer Youth Workers
Up Close and Personal: How to Build Community in Your Youth Group
Youth Ministry Nuts and Bolts
The Youth Specialties Handbook for Great Camps and Retreats
Youth Specialties Clip Art Book
Youth Specialties Clip Art Book, Volume 2

How to Survive Middle School

A humorous guide to the wonder years

Rick Bundschuh

from

Youth Specialties

ZondervanPublishingHouse
A Division of HarperCollins*Publishers*

How to Survive Middle School

Copyright ©1991 by Youth Specialties, Inc.

Youth Specialties Books, 1224 Greenfield Drive, El Cajon, California 92021, are published by Zondervan Publishing House, Grand Rapids, Michigan 49530

Library of Congress Cataloging-in-Publication Data

Bundschuh, Rick, 1951-
      How to survive middle school: a humorous guide to the wonder
      years / Rick Bundschuh.
      p.   cm. — (Get 'em Growing) "Youth Specialties."
      Summary: A guide for young people entering middle school,
      which covers such things as getting lost, where to find help, ad-
      justing to home room, etc.
      ISBN 0-310-53521-2
      1. Middle school students—United States—Conduct of life—
      Juvenile literature. 2. Middle schools—United States—Juvenile
      literature. [1. Middle schools. 2. Schools. 3. Conduct of life.]
I. Title. II. Series.
LB1135.B85 1991
373.2'36—dc20   90-47415
                                              CIP
                                             AC

All Scripture quotations, unless otherwise noted, are taken from the *Holy Bible: New International Version* (North American Edition). Copyright ©1973, 1978, 1984 by the International Bible Society. Used by permission of Zondervan Bible Publishers.

Edited by Leslie Emmons and Kathi George
Design and typography by Mark Rayburn
Illustrated by Rick Bundschuh

Printed in the United States of America

92 93 94 95 96 97 98 99 / CH / 10 9 8 7 6 5 4 3 2

About the YOUTHSOURCE™ Publishing Group

YOUTHSOURCE™ books, tapes, videos, and other resources pool the expertise of three of the finest youth ministry resource providers in the world:

➤ **Campus Life Books**—publishers of the award-winning *Campus Life* magazine, who for nearly fifty years have helped high schoolers live Christian lives.

➤ **Youth Specialties**—serving ministers to middle school, junior high, and high school youth for over twenty years through books, magazines, and training events such as the National Youth Workers Convention.

➤ **Zondervan Publishing House**—one of the oldest, largest, and most respected evangelical Christian publishers in the world.

———————————

Campus Life
465 Gundersen Dr.
Carol Stream, IL 60188
708/260-6200

Youth Specialties
1224 Greenfield Dr.
El Cajon, CA 92021
619/440-2333

Zondervan
1415 Lake Dr. S.E.
Grand Rapids, MI 49506
616/698-6900

To Mike Furukawa . . . a
junior higher forever.

TABLE OF CONTENTS

Hey! Read this first!

My name is Justin Bundschuh. I'm 13 years old and I have been through all the things in this book. My dad is the author and I'd like to tell you a little of what I thought about what he wrote. This book is for you to find out what to look forward to: like locker rooms, new people, and school lunches (yecch). I think this book will be a good guide for middle school because all the stuff you need to know is in here and it's even put in a funny way.

I gave my dad a little advice in writing it because middle school was a long time ago for him. I hope you enjoy it, so read on!

Justin Bundschuh
Kauai, Hawaii

INTRODUCTION

This book is for those of you who are starting your journey through middle school or junior high school. I'd like to think that it can be used like a map through a mine field is used. It won't keep you from stomping on a nice, juicy land mine, if that's what you really want to do, but at least it will show you where most of the land mines are hidden, if you decide to avoid them. Most of the problems that kids get themselves into during middle school can be dodged if you know where to step.

I hope that some of the questions, concerns, and doubts that you have about entering this new adventure will be answered as you read through this book. All the stories are true, even the bizarre ones. I have changed the names of the kids involved, 'cause that's what you're supposed to do when you write a book.

Throughout, you will find that I use the term *middle school* instead of junior high school. For the sake of simplicity, I had to decide what to call the time you spend in school between the sixth and ninth grades. For those of

you who have never heard of a middle school, it's just like a junior high, except that it starts with sixth grade instead of seventh, and ends with eighth grade instead of ninth.

I wrote this book because I have many friends who are just starting middle school and who are concerned about what will happen to them. I'd like to consider you my friend, too. If you have questions about middle school that are not answered in this book, please write to me. I'll be glad to help if I can.

Most of all, I hope this book helps you to see that God can be your friend and guide through the wild years ahead of you.

Rick Bundschuh
P.O. Box 633
Lawai, HI 96765

CHAPTER 1

Getting Started

I barfed in class. During the first week of first grade, in front of everybody. There I was, busy painting fine works of art. I thought I could hold it back. I was wrong. I puked all over my piece of art (adding far more color, but ruining its resale value). My breakfast rolled down the painting, through the paint tray, and into a puddle on the floor. Everyone stared at the mess for a minute, and then the laughter began—it started with the jug-eared kid in the back of the class and rippled out across the room.

Trudging to the health office, I couldn't believe what had happened. I was crushed, humiliated. The churning in my gut could not compete with the cloud of doom that now hung over me. I knew my life was ruined.

Since that horrible day, I have managed to pull myself back together. But even so, I have faced every new school year and every move to a new school with a sense of dread.

Jangled Nerves

It's natural to feel nervous when you face a new experience. And middle school is definitely something new. Lots of kids wonder, "What terrible things are going to happen to me? Will I do or say something that will prove to everyone else that I'm a geek?"

The stuff in this book will not keep you from barfing—stomachs will do what they must—but it may help you deal with some of the other things that worry you. It will help you know what to expect, what to do, and in some cases, what to avoid doing.

If you're like I was, your very first day of school will probably be scary, so I've written a whole chapter about it. Interested? Let's get started.

The Big Day

When your electric alarm clock buzzes obnoxiously that first morning, you'll already be awake. In fact, I doubt that you'll have gotten much sleep at all, what with thinking about this day. *The first day of school.* Most likely, you'll be experiencing some high anxiety. Take a deep breath and try to relax. Chances are that you'll not only survive this new adventure, you'll enjoy it too—once you get the hang of it.

The first clue that your life is changing will hit you before you even leave your house—the uncomfortable feel of stiff new clothes. When you walk on campus, look around and you'll see that just about everyone is experiencing it: blue jeans are so stiff that they can stand up by themselves, and tennis shoes are so squeaky clean that they don't yet attract flies. Colors are brilliant, ketchup stains are absent—and some kids are even walking around with price tags still dangling from their clothes!

Naturally, everyone is trying to make a good first impression. You may feel like laughing at their efforts, but it is important for you to realize that if you come to school on the first day wearing last year's leftovers, you'll feel like a middle school hobo. So wear your best and be careful not to spill stuff on your new clothes . . . at least today.

Lost in a Crowd

When you get to school, you'll be surrounded by people you've never met. That's because a bunch of elementary schools feed into one middle school. Everybody will be spending a lot of time checking everyone else out. Try not to let this process bother you—you'll probably be doing a bit of checking for yourself! Some kids are overjoyed at the thought of having so many cute boys or girls to choose from. Others worry a bit that they will not be as important in this sea of faces as they were in their comfortable little grade schools.

You may be convinced that you will start your first day by doing something that makes you look like a complete jerk. Let me reassure you—almost everybody feels self-conscious and out of place, but don't expect them to admit it. And relax—big blunders rarely happen on the first day. You'll have the rest of the school year to make a jerk out of yourself.

Scrambled Schedules

Now that you're used to being looked over, it's time to find out where you're supposed to be and get there. (Well, maybe you had better find the bathrooms first.) In middle school you will be assigned a new class, a new room, a new subject, and a new teacher for every hour of the school day.

Some schools mail your class schedules to you during the summer. Others simply hang computer printouts listing student names and their classroom assignments on hallway bulletin boards, and some schools post notices that direct you to your *homeroom,* and your homeroom teacher hands you your schedule.

If you have a common last name, things can get really confusing at this point. The poor kid whose last name happens to be *Smith* can end up wandering the halls all day, looking for classes that really belong to some other *Smith.* This can get really upsetting if you find you have been assigned to a boys' gym class . . . and you're a girl! If this happens, don't panic and go home. Help is available, and with any luck, your problem will be solved by the end of the semester.

Oh—and one last piece of advice about schedules—write yours down in a notebook, just in case you misplace the copy you are handed. If you think you might lose your notebook, write your schedule on your arm. Hopefully, you won't lose that.

Finding Your Way

The *fear of getting lost* rates right up there with *the fear of throwing up in the cafeteria.* And if you get lost shopping at the mall, maybe there is a reason to feel a bit nervous. But chances are, you won't get lost at all. Oh, there may be moments of panic, but little genuine "lostness."

The worst that can happen is that you'll stumble into a class after it has already started. If you enjoy drawing attention to yourself, this won't be a big deal, but if you're trying to develop a low-key, cool image, the experience may be very embarrassing. The best you can do is to try to look calm—otherwise everyone will know that you have been desperately wandering the halls.

Help Wanted

When you needed help in grade school, you could always ask an adult. Adults were easy to spot because they were so much taller than everyone else. But in middle school, finding an adult by size alone is a bit harder since some kids are already about as tall as their teachers. This means that for you to get an adult's help, you will have to find someone who looks old or who is wearing a tie.

If you're really lost, one place that is usually full of adults is the office. You can always go there and ask for help without feeling terribly stupid. There's no reason to feel ashamed about going to the office if you can't figure out where you're supposed to be . . . after all, your friends will be in there asking for help, too!

If you'd rather not make trips to the office between all of your classes, take heart—you still have other options. One is to follow a friend around. If that friend has figured out the system, you're in luck. If not, at least you'll be lost together. Or you can team up with someone who is one grade above you in school and have that person guide you through the day. Be careful—some enterprising older kid may charge you for your tour.

First Class

Your first class of the morning is usually identified as your homeroom. Before you crack open your books, the teacher will take roll, read the announcements, and tell you about any upcoming events.

Expect the seating in every class to be about the same. Teachers rarely assign seats, and most of the time, finding seats turns into a free-for-all. You can almost predict where different kids will sit—the dummies will race for the seats farthest back in the class (where they can carve on their desks all year long) and the brains will look for desks right up front. And everyone will sit as far away as possible from the kid who stepped in doggy doo on his way to school!

Logic will tell you that if you want the seat of your choice, you should get to class as soon as possible on the first day. But actual experience will probably teach you that you'll just have to take whatever seat is left after you've explored the whole school trying to find your class.

Bell Ringers

You'll know class has begun when the school bell rings. In fact, you'll probably find that your actions in middle school are all directed by bells. They will tell you when to eat, study, change classes, and go home. If you forget what to do when the bell rings, just follow everybody else and you'll probably be okay.

Locker Battles

Middle school students store their books, jackets, lunches, and other junk in lockers. In some schools, lockers are assigned to students. In others, you can choose any locker that has not already been claimed by someone else, and this might be a good reason to get your mom to drive you to school early on the first day.

If you have a choice, take a top locker rather than a bottom one. It seems like every time a kid with a lower locker kneels to get into it, the slob above him opens his door and unleashes an avalanche of books and papers on his head. And then as he recovers and staggers to his feet, the guy closes his locker and adds a nasty dent to the poor kid's skull.

If your school has lockers without built-in locks, you will have to bring a lock from home. Pay attention when you are told what kind to bring—combination locks seem to be the usual. You'll feel pretty dorky being the only kid with a cheapo brand key lock hanging from your locker.

It's typical to lock your combination inside your locker and then forget the combination. Unfortunately, it's also expensive, because the school janitor then has to cut the lock off with huge snippers, all so that you can get to your combination . . . which you suddenly will no longer need. You can avoid being typical by writing your combination on your arm. Or you can write it in pencil on your neighbor's locker like everyone else does.

One of your friends may want to share lockers with you. It is often best for your friendship to refuse. Sharing makes it tough to fit all of your junk in. Not to mention the fact that you may find your friend uses more than just your locker.

Picky Particulars

As you go from class to class, your teachers will undoubtedly give special instructions. Since your day is going to be so baffling, you probably won't remember anything you are told to do from one class to the next. This is the time to get out your trusty pencil and write down the stuff your teacher tells you.

For example, in some classes you'll get books and be told to put covers on them. In other classes you'll be asked to bring a certain item with you every day. If you learn to write down the various instructions you are given, it will help you to come to class prepared. That is, as long as you remember to take home the notebook you've made your notes in!

Lonely Lunches

Now it's time for lunch. If you go to a large middle school, you may be surprised to find that there are several lunch times. You may be scheduled to eat during first lunch, while all your friends are assigned to the second lunch period. Don't bother to complain—the bad news is that most school administrators will shed few tears over the fact that you must eat alone and will not agree to switching your lunch time. Look around and try to make new friends.

Pepto-Bismol, Please

Have you ever wondered where all that leftover food that you tell your parents to send to the starving kids in Africa really goes? Well, now you know. It ends up in the school cafeteria.

I don't think anyone who has gone through middle school has ever actually *liked* school cafeteria food. It is eaten strictly to avoid starvation. If you can't stomach what is served, you can always bring food from home. Just don't carry it in a lunch box. No matter what kind of cute graphics are on your lunch box, they will be considered dumb looking. A standard brown paper bag has been the traditional school lunch accessory for years.

Notorious Teachers

You'll learn things about many of your teachers before you even enter their classrooms. Sometimes these facts will be spread during lunch time by students who have just come from a certain class, but more often they will come from older kids who have already had a certain teacher.

Try to keep an open mind about all of your teachers. Some are labeled *crummy* or *mean* by featherheads in their classes who want to goof off and aren't able to get away with it. You may really enjoy a teacher that everybody else dislikes.

Unearned Reputations

If you have older brothers or sisters, you may be pegged before you even get to school. Obviously, this isn't fair. But if your sister was a math wiz and you can't add four to four without a calculator, be prepared to hear your math teacher say, "Well, Junior, it's going to be great having another brilliant student from the Jones family." And try not to gag.

The situation is even worse if you have an older brother or sister who was a troublemaker. It gets humiliating being sent to the vice principal's office every day, simply because you share your family's name with a big brother or sister who is a jerk.

Naked Kids

A major fear of many new middle school students is the need to get undressed and take group showers in physical education (P.E.) class. If this fear has haunted you, it's about to become a reality. Most schools do not have private dressing rooms. In fact, you may feel like a longhorn steer as you are herded through the shower stalls.

Expect to be very uncomfortable at first—not only with your own body, but also with that fact that, unless you have lived in a nudist colony, you will never have seen so many naked people before in your whole life!

Some kids try to put off the inevitable by wearing their P.E. uniforms under their school clothes, by refusing to suit up for class, or by skipping showers (thereby blessing everyone who gets too close with the sour smell of body odor). Even though you may not be happy about communal showering, this is another change that you will have to swallow hard and accept. In a couple of weeks it won't seem so bad.

One Last Word

Well, we've covered most of the things that you will experience on the first day. The one thing that you probably won't experience—and you may have feared it—is getting into a beef with some other kid. Take heart. On the first day, even school bullies are too busy getting lost to spend much time picking on other kids. Give them a day or two to adjust and then they'll come around to pick on you.

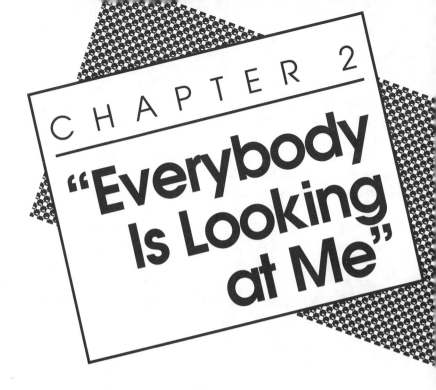

CHAPTER 2

"Everybody Is Looking at Me"

John was a smiling, likable kid. He had thick, curly hair, a square head connected to a pudgy body, and two false front teeth. John took great pleasure in clicking these teeth out at girls and watching them groan and scream. He seemed to favor two or three shirts, and his shoelaces were always untied. John sat in front of me during social studies, and John was my friend.

But that didn't stop me from taping a sign that read "KICK ME" to his back. For an entire morning, good ol' John dodged flying feet. Suddenly the center of attention, he had all the other kids coming up to him, telling him, "Okay!" and hauling off with swift kicks.

The fun ended in math class when John trudged through a gauntlet of extended feet and the teacher, instead of granting the wish taped to his back, removed it. Naturally, everyone thought the joke was quite funny. That is, everyone except John! But failing to see the humor in his situation didn't stop him from trying the same stunt on a kid who sat in front of him in English.

For a short while, John was the joke of the school, a fate that most of us fear. It's natural to want to be liked and accepted. No one wants to be thought of as bizarre—unless being bizarre is the only way to get attention. We want to be thought of as people others want to get to know. In fact, your desire to be liked and accepted is stronger now than it will be at any other point in your life.

Sticks and Stones

Unfortunately, many of your middle school "friends" will be radically cutting and cruel . . . all in fun, of course. Something you do, say, or even look like will be enough to set them howling for days or to brand you with a nickname impossible to shake. In most circumstances, the only options you'll have will be to change friends, become a hermit, or bravely take the jibes with a forced smile. To blubber and cry or to explode in anger will only make you more fun to tease. People love a reaction.

Most of the time it will be the people who like you that will take advantage of your slipups. One kid in our youth group was named Mike. That is, everyone *called* him Mike until he fell asleep once on a long car trip. Because of his allergies, Mike had gotten in the habit of sleeping with his mouth open. Not a problem at home in his own bed, but this time he had an audience and worse yet, he started to drool. He drooled down his chin, along his neck, and all over the side of the car seat. The scene prompted loud hoots and howls of laughter from all of his pals in the car. He was immediately christened "Droolbucket." The name stuck all the way through high school. I like to imagine the look that crossed some father's face when his daughter told him that she was going to the prom with Droolbucket.

Another seventh grader in this same group had hands with long, bony fingers. After studying them, one of his friends decided that they looked like monkey hands. So the kid—whose real name even *I* can't remember—was nicknamed "Cheetah" after the chimp in the old Tarzan movies. He's still called by that name.

I don't want to alarm you, but if you have a large nose, freckles, eyes of two different colors, webbed toes, or an outie belly-button, you're in for some comments. The most likely kind? "Hey, did you know you have a big nose?" or "How'd you get so many freckles?" and similar brilliant questions or comments. If you're clever, you can always think up some snappy comebacks and have them ready for instant use. For example, someone asks, "How'd you get so many freckles?" You can smartly reply, "I was getting a tan under a screen door, how'd you think?"

Name Games

If there's nothing too unusual about your looks, the gang may have some fun with your name. Kids love to twist other people's names into millions of variations. You're in real trouble if your name can take on some kind of meaning. In our school we had a film about child molesters. The villain's name was Ralph. Pity the poor kid who also bore that name! He got hassled mercilessly for weeks. When fellow students saw him coming, they would shout in mock terror, "Eeek! It's *Ralph*! Run away, run away!"

There was one kid who never got direct comments about his last name, even though it was a classic. His name was Brian Butt—*no kidding*! He was huge, twice as big as anyone else in the class—which, of course, explains why no one made fun of him to his face.

Being picked on a little bit is part of life, and you've got to learn to take some abuse. I realize that sometimes what people say hurts. Jokes can get old in a hurry and some guys just don't know when to stop giving others a hard time. But the truth is, the fact that you drool in your sleep, have a big nose, or have Mooselips for a last name does not make you a winner or a loser. That is decided by the kind of person you are on the inside.

Teaming Up

You may find yourself in situations that are tougher to deal with than having people make fun of your name or your kite-sized ears. One of these situations often comes up in P.E. class. Coaches frequently choose team captains and then let these jocks choose their teammates. What this means is that some punk is going to decide whether or not you will be the last player chosen—a humiliating experience. Only those who have been picked last really understand the feelings of rejection this creates.

If you are ever chosen last, you'll have to decide how to respond. Allow the fact that people don't think much of your athletic ability to make you feel like a failure, and you'll miss a whole bundle of great things about yourself. Perhaps you do other things better than you kick footballs. It's possible that you will be the one who gets good grades in algebra or who blazes away on a musical instrument few others can play. The fact that you aren't athletic is minor in comparison!

Try to avoid feeling bitter toward those who make you feel unwanted. And by all means, avoid using your science class to build bombs for their lockers!

Like many other things in life, you can't control what others do to you, but you can control what you do to others. If you're reading this book and have never been picked last for a team, you have a great opportunity to make someone else's day a bit better. Try going up to your team captain as he is choosing players and suggest that he not leave "ol' butterfingers" for last this time. Unless your team leader is a complete peanuthead, he will probably go for your idea. Even if you think he won't, it's worth trying. The smile and surprise you'll see on the poor klutz's face will stay with you for a lifetime.

Fleeting Childhood

Many kids struggle with the feeling that they must either give up all the fun stuff and toys of childhood or have people make rude jokes about them and call them babies. It's true that as we become adults we get rid of childish things, but hey, you're still a kid! All that's happening is that you're moving on to a more sophisticated level of play.

Sooner or later you'll have to put the toys of your past behind you, but it's okay to feel sad about that. You're mourning a passage from one stage of life to another. And don't be in a big hurry to stop messing around with what other kids may label "toys." Play with your stuff at home, in private, and nobody will give you a hard time. You'll be grown up for most of your life, so enjoy being a kid while you can.

A Healthy Self-Image

Experiences in middle school can shake your self confidence and make you wish you were someone else. You may become discouraged about your looks, your athletic ability, or your lack of popularity. You may wish for money to buy the clothes or goodies that some other kids seem to have in such abundance. Or perhaps you'll feel embarrassed about your parents and wonder if there's any place where you can trade them in for a new, more understanding set. And you may not really be too happy even with the real you.

If you find yourself having these feelings, please consider the fact that God doesn't make junk. When God made you, he didn't misread the ingredient list or throw in the ugly stick. He made you purposefully–*yes, big nose and all*! In fact, God created you to be more than a mediocre, semi-dull, average, middle-class person: he created you to be *great*.

Great? Yeah, but not in the same way that rock stars and famous politicians are great. He created you to be great in *his* way. Jesus often said things like, ". . . whoever wants to become great among you must be your servant" (Matthew 20:26). He repeated himself a number of times, explaining to people how they could be important, how they could be somebodies in their homes, at their schools, and in their work situations. He gave strange prescriptions, like "the first shall be last" and "Whoever wants to be great . . . must be the servant of all" (see Luke 13:30 and Mark 10:43).

Many people have a hard time making sense of Christ's words. They sound like hocus-pocus nonsense. The famous writer, G. K. Chesterton, put Christ's teaching into less puzzling words. He said, "The great man is the man who makes every man feel great."[1] This is important for you to understand, especially if you sometimes feel like a bug splat on the windshield of life. To be popular and likable, you must forget about pleasing yourself and work on making other people feel important and likable.

Let me give you an example of how this works. Suppose you and a bunch of your friends are talking about what a wizard you are on a snowboard. In turn, almost all of the kids are describing great moves they've made or massive wipeouts they've survived. In a way, you're a bunch of braggarts trying to outdo each other with bigger and better stories, hoping that someone is listening and being impressed.

To make someone else feel great in this situation, make a true but positive comment about the snowboarding ability of a beginner in the group. It's a gift. A free, uplifting note in a bull session. But you'll be amazed at what it will do to warm the heart of your beginner friend. And in turn the friend you have complimented will see you in a slightly new, slightly more valuable light. You will have started to become great in his eyes.

One Last Word

What Jesus says is true. The way to become great is to stop feeling sorry for yourself or wishing to be somebody else and to start giving kindness and attention to others. With just a moment's reflection, you'll see how this works in your own life. Think for a moment about the adults who mean the most to you right now. They are probably the ones who pay attention to you or give you encouragement. They may be your parents, a teacher, a coach, or a youth worker or minister. But you like them because they like *you*.

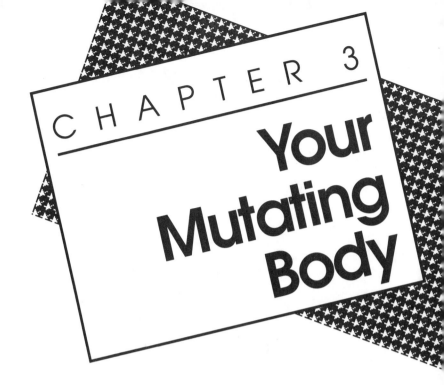

CHAPTER 3

Your Mutating Body

Josh landed in boys' choir. It certainly was not his first choice. He would have preferred to be in art, wood-shop, metalshop . . . any class but choir. Unfortunately, all of those other classes were filled and Josh was told that he would have to wait until the end of the semester for a transfer. So for the moment, he was in boys' choir. But Josh was not alone. Boys' choir was the dumping ground for all of the overloaded elective courses at the school.

His teacher was a plump, highly emotional woman named Mrs. Hutton. I don't know how much this woman was paid to lead boys' choir, but it couldn't have been enough. Trying to control a bunch of unwilling recruits and getting some semblance of music from their foul lips is deserving of combat pay.

During the first week of school, Mrs. Hutton tested the boys' voices to find out where they would fit into her master plan for turning rabble into a musical miracle. Josh was forced to sing a short solo. Red-faced, he quietly breathed out his lines in a lofty and sweet soprano voice (. . . uh, this is the high end of the musical range for those of you without a drop of musical knowledge). But weird events were in store for Josh and his friends.

As Josh tried to hit some of the notes in the songs the choir was practicing, his voice would crack without warning and tumble from lilting heights to some lower depths that sounded harsh and tuneless. Josh's voice was changing. By the time Josh was able to transfer into a shop class, he was singing in the baritone section of the choir. His voice dropped three octaves in a few months' time. So common was this situation that Mrs. Hutton's soprano section was down to a couple of kids by the end of the year.

A Period of Changes

Welcome to the time of life during which your body does whatever it wants, when it wants, without notifying you! Have you ever watched an old Wolfman movie? The sweet, lovable guy turns into a hairy monster when the moon is full. Well, this is kind of what's happening to you, only you are changing a bit more slowly and with a little luck will not end up quite as hairy.

You are changing from a kid into an adult, mutating from what everyone called the freckle-faced, goofy-looking twerp of the block into something yet unknown. Although you may not notice how quickly this is happening, you can be sure that Aunt Bertha will comment on it at the next family gathering.

There are a few facts about this period of change that will be important for you to remember. First of all, please keep in mind that, sooner or later, everybody experiences this mutation; nobody gets left out. No matter how skinny, flat, hairless, short, or baby-faced you are, dramatic changes are on the way.

But the next fact is just as important: Bodies change at different speeds. Some kids you know will be huge, hairy monsters or shapely beauties by seventh grade. And you may even find yourself part of this group. Others will change very little. You may have guessed that some kids who are late bloomers are self-conscious about being small and hairless, but you may be surprised to learn that many of those who grow quickly feel just as weird. They fail to see their early development as a good thing because it makes them different from other kids.

And did you know that bodies often develop or grow unevenly? For example, a boy's legs may grow so quickly and so out of proportion with the rest of his body that he becomes clumsy. A girl may find that one breast grows a little faster than the other one, or that she grows everywhere but in her bust line. Relax. Things will sort themselves out eventually.

Physical changes often affect your eating habits. You may develop a huge appetite and feel hungry all of the time—but remember: you're trying to feed a mutating body. If you find that your stomach insists on growling in class, demanding food, get in the habit of carrying extra fruit or cheese in your lunch to use for snacks. Sometimes chewing gum can silence a noisy gut, too.

Sometimes a growth spurt will cause pain in your arms or legs. These experiences are normal but uncomfortable. Be comforted by the thought that they will eventually go away, leaving you with a mature physique.

Measures of Maturity

Just because a kid happens to look older than everyone else in his or her class does not mean that he or she *is* more mature. Maturity is far more a measure of what is on the inside than it is a measure of what is on the outside. And though you may be tempted to envy those kids in grown-up bodies, developing early is not always best for you in the long run. It wasn't in Tami's case.

Tami was already developing curves in elementary school. By the time she hit eighth grade she looked like a young woman, not a kid in middle school. Other girls envied her. Boys would whisper their thoughts about her body to each other as she passed by.

But because she looked older, Tami attracted older boys—boys who drove cars rather than riding skateboards or bikes. Tami was fascinated by their attention, and they were taken with her gorgeous body. Before long, Tami was pregnant. Because her parents were Christians, they decided that she should not have an abortion. Tami dropped out of school until after the baby was born, put the baby up for adoption, and transferred to another school district.

Tami's physical maturity caused problems because she appeared older on the outside than she really was on the inside. The sex vultures in any community spot these early bloomers in a hurry and are quick to devour them!

Barry's case was not so tragic. He simply reached physical maturity before anyone else. By eighth grade he could grow a full beard, much to the envy of the other guys who would have ruptured themselves trying to squeeze one shavable hair from their chins. But it's often true that those who get it first, lose it first. No, Barry didn't lose the hair on his face. That stayed nice and healthy. But Barry was bald by the time he was twenty-one!

And Tami, the curvy eighth grader? She was in her prime during middle school. From then on, it was all downhill. The funny thing is that all those thin, flat, scrawny, underdeveloped boys and girls who are not much to look at in middle school often blossom suddenly in high school . . . much to everyone's delight.

If you are an early bloomer, your situation is far from hopeless. I've told two stories that may leave you a bit concerned. Take heart. Kids who physically mature early do not always find themselves in a crummy situation. In fact, during middle school there can be some real great things you can do to take advantage of being bigger or more developed than most everyone else. Here are a couple of suggestions.

Get Involved in Sports. This is your chance to be a real superstar. You can probably outrun, outjump, and outswim most of the little squirts you compete with. Being involved with sports is also a good way to expend energy and stay out of trouble.

Develop Leadership Skills. It's a curious fact, but in middle school many kids tend to look up to somebody they uh, . . . *have* to look up to. This is a chance to be a leader, not a follower. It is also a chance to be a hero, since the school bully will seldom want to tangle with someone bigger than he is. You can become a "body-guard" for smaller friends who are getting picked on.

Even though you may be looking mature in your body, don't let that stop you from acting your age. Avoid the pressure to "be as grown up as you look." Enjoy being a kid—you won't get to be one again!

Changing Emotions

Most girls have their first period during middle school. It can take a while for your body to fall into a regular twenty-eight-day cycle. To avoid any unpleasant accidents, always carry an extra pad or tampon in your purse in case your period decides to surprise you and start up during school. With these periods may also come some discomfort, grouchiness, and lack of energy. Be sensitive to your body's need for more rest and realize that this is not a good time to be making important decisions. And if one of your friends acts unusually moody, try not to take her seriously. She'll probably be a new person in a few days.

Smelly Subjects

And now for a bit of bad news. Very soon, your body is going to start stinking. Yeah, I'm talking serious B.O. and foot rot. In every junior high group, there is one kid who still hasn't gotten the message about using deodorant and taking showers. His teeth are green from yesterday's lunch, his feet smell like they've been dead inside his shoes for a month, and visible fumes seep out from under his arms. The only kids who will sit next to him are the ones with such bad head colds that they can't notice the

foul aroma swirling around them.

You see, when you were a little kid, you could sweat up a storm and smell slightly stale at the worst. But once the changes that move you towards adulthood begin, stale is replaced with stink. This is where good *hygiene* (cleanliness) comes in. You're going to have to shower thoroughly, use B.O. juice (deodorant), brush and floss your teeth, and change your socks and underwear *every day*. Otherwise, you'll get a label that you don't want. And besides, you'll find that it is much easier to talk others into allowing you in a crowded car if you smell decent!

Another little pleasure that some kids experience is dandruff. You've seen people with snowstorms of flakes on their shoulders. It's gross *and* avoidable. The solution? Wash your hair every day. If your scalp tends to be flaky, use a dandruff shampoo. Unless you have some special skin problem, this should take care of any flakiness.

Blemish Blues

Probably the worst plague you may face will be the sudden emergence of zits. A clear, sweet face can look like a battlefield with eyeballs almost overnight. Blackheads, pimples, and zits are caused by the sudden increase of oils in and on your skin. When oils, dirt, and grime collect on your face, find their way into your pores, and clog them, they create blackheads. When pores get infected or irritated, they turn into gnarly and sometimes painful pimples. Zits are somewhat related to what you eat (oily foods and chocolate), but they are usually controllable by scrubbing your face with soap, water, and a washcloth.

Some people see pimples as the end of the world. They are sure that everyone notices the nasty things. The truth is that unless a zit is the size of Mount Saint Helens, it probably won't be noticed at all. But people *will* notice if you take such lousy care of your skin that you get a zit farm going. If you find a zit on your face, don't pick at it, especially if your fingers are dirty. It will only make the bugger look worse. It can also cause a more serious infection. Obviously, if you have a big white ball of pus hanging from the end of your nose, you've got to get rid of it. Just make sure that you sanitize anything that will touch your face. Rubbing alcohol works well. Think of yourself as a doctor doing minor surgery.

Acne is another nasty complexion problem that may affect you as you move through your changes. This skin condition looks a lot like zits gone wild. It can spread from your face to your back and it is hard to control. If your parents struggled with acne, you probably will, too. Although some people first have trouble with acne in their twenties or during a pregnancy, most people find that it is at its worst during the teenage years.

Acne is very difficult to control without help. Naturally, it helps to keep your face clean, but if you think you're getting acne, you may need to see a special skin doctor known as a dermatologist. Dermatologists can prescribe special medicines and treatments to help control acne. Severe cases can scar your face for life, so don't mess around. See a doctor.

Brace Face

By this point in life, most kids have lost their baby teeth and have their permanent ones. And a lot of the

time, these permanent teeth are crooked. For this reason, you'll see a lot of kids with braces on their teeth in middle school.

If you find yourself enduring braces, you may feel very ashamed of your appearance and may even try to smile without showing your teeth. Don't bother. Braces have become so common that most kids won't even notice whether you are wearing them or not.

Thank your folks for spending loads of money so that you can have a nice smile—and keep away from strong magnets.

The Opposite Sex

Of all the changes you'll experience during middle school, none will be as noticeable to you as the changes you experience sexually. As you mutate from child to adult, you may be shocked to discover hair growing in some very private places. Boys sometimes experience *wet dreams* at night (when your penis ejaculates semen) or erections at embarrassing moments. Girls, who are often a little ahead of boys at this stage of development, may find themselves daydreaming about getting married to some kid in school or about attracting male attention.

When you were a little kid you probably thought that the opposite sex had cooties, was stupid, or was a waste of time. You might have been curious about what the other sex looks like under all those clothes, but it never interested you as it may now during middle school.

I'll tell you more about what you can expect from these feelings in another chapter, but here I need to say this: The fascination that you may feel towards a member of the opposite sex is normal. It's like hunger. There's a time and place for it, just like meal time is the time and place for satisfying the hunger for food. God tells us that we need to control our sexual urges until the time is right. And God knows what he is talking about!

Again, because we all develop at varying speeds, don't feel that you are weird if you don't experience any of what I've just described until you hit high school. There's no such thing as normal . . . everyone is abnormal at this time of life.

All in all, the changes that you go through physically during your middle school years are amazing. You may outgrow your clothes every few months, discover new emotions and feelings, and be astonished that you look so little like a kid and so much like an adult. But there is one thing that you can be sure of: God didn't make a mistake when he made you. He hasn't forgotten you, nor has he played a dirty trick on you! You will not mutate into an alien or some kind of a huge toad. You will slowly become a mature man or woman.

So relax and enjoy the process. Be yourself, even if you find that your body is maturing more slowly or more quickly than you would like. In other words, forget the padded bra!

Safety First

Keep in mind that you only get one body in this life and that it's your job to take care of it. If you are reckless on your bike or skateboard, you will leave large amounts of skin on the sidewalk. Take precautions and wear knee pads and helmets. And don't think you are made out of rubber, because you're not! Be a little cautious—the life you risk is your own.

Don't do stuff like tattooing or intentionally scarring your body. You may regret it later in life. Don't experiment with things obviously harmful to your body—things like drugs, alcohol, and tobacco. Remember that every smoker who dies of lung cancer started out thinking that he or she would beat the odds . . . and didn't. What I'm trying to tell you, is to do the best you can to keep your body in good shape and God will do his best to make sure you end up with a final product that both of you will be happy with.

One Last Word

Here's a word of wisdom that comes from my mother. She told me when I was a growing kid, "The only thing you should stick in your ear is your elbow."

CHAPTER 4

The Campus Zoo

In some ways going to middle school is like going to the zoo, because a whole collection of different species exist on campus. Each one has its own gathering place: one crew dominates the steps, another congregates in the north corner of the football field, and still another group meets under a big tree. And just like the critters at the zoo, they leave their marks behind: Coke cans and Twinkie wrappers litter some sites, names carved in wood or stone or dug out of the grass are found in others, and cigarette butts still smolder on the ground at the far end of the campus.

Often each group will dress and talk differently from all the others. If you don't look and talk like the kids in a particular group, you won't be allowed to hang out with them. In fact, they will consider you to be at the same level as a maggot.

These groups also dominate different areas of the cafeteria or lunch court during feeding time. Pity the poor kid from one species who tries to eat in another's territory. At the least, stares and growls will make it clear that he or she is not welcome.

Most of these little clusters have a ringleader, a small group of disciples or *toadies* who find pleasure in serving the ringleader, and varying numbers of "wannabes," or fringe members. And just as in the animal kingdom, the ringleader is most often the largest or most physically mature kid in the group.

If you don't yet belong to a group, you will feel pressured to find a group with which to hang out. This is natural and really very important because we all need to feel that we fit in and are liked.

Almost every middle school houses the same *kinds* of species. Hairstyles, slang words, music, and fashions may change, but the nature of the groups always remain the same. Use the following list of species to prepare yourself for what you will find on your campus. Your school may not have all of these groups and subgroups, but it will have many of them and maybe some others I haven't mentioned—species may mutate even before this book comes off the press!

Bullies

This species is the most feared by those entering middle school. Although bullies do exist, they are usually of little threat to new students—unless a newcomer accidentally trips one! Usually bullies are bigger, meaner,

and nastier than the rest of the student population. Bullies are also dumber and think they are cooler because they can beat up on everyone else. People may fear bullies, but few people like them.

The best way to deal with bullies is to avoid them. Walk the other way and don't make wise comments or give them any reasons to show you who's boss. If you find it difficult to walk away from tense situations, make friends with someone who will come to your rescue when you're picked on. Most big goons don't want to mess with those who might take them down in a fight.

I know that in your wildest fantasies you are able to stand up to a mean, drooling, wart-faced bully and beat him to a pancake. Unless you have a black-belt in some oriental martial art, just remember that your thoughts are fantasy!

Strangely enough, sometimes small tough kids will start acting like bullies, maybe to make up for their size. These kids have to choose their victims carefully or their life expectancies will be shorter than they are!

Girl Bullies

In some schools you will find that girls also go around acting tough and picking fights. Most kids in middle school think that watching a couple of girls fight is highly entertaining—probably because some girls fight dirty: pulling hair, scratching, and biting as well as hitting. The rules for dealing with male bullies also apply for female ones: ignore them, and don't allow yourself to be pushed into a fight.

Jocks and Jockettes

This group is made up of sports freaks. They usually love baseball, football, soccer, volleyball, basketball . . . in fact, just about any sport in which players run around and get sweaty. Often this group has many of the larger students in the school, and jocks are rarely pushed around or hassled. They also have lots of photos of themselves in the school yearbook.

You might have assumed that jockettes are girls who play sports, but they're not: they're the girls who hang around with jocks. Many of them are future cheerleaders and are very pretty. And they won't give you the time of day unless you are a jock.

Substrata Athletes

This species can be found in almost every school. They are the kids who participate in sports not sponsored or recognized by the school but recognized by everyone else. Sometimes substrata athletes and the girls who hang out with them or who participate in the same sports are even more popular than the jocks and jockettes.

Substrata sports are often determined by region. Schools near the ocean will have surfers and body-boarders (also called "sponge riders"), licking the salt off themselves in first period from a session before school. In mountainous areas you'll find skiers and snowboarders hanging out together, discussing their most daring feats. In other areas you may find cowpokes wearing boots and hats to school. These boys are happiest wrestling bulls to the ground. Almost every school has skateboarders creating havoc on whatever concrete they can find and bleeding on their desks from unhealed sidewalk skids. And, no doubt, at a school in some remote corner of the globe, a group of trapeze artists hangs out together.

Headbangers

Headbangers are the kids in any middle school that favor giving adults shock treatment. They play the noisiest music possible at full volume on their stereos, wear clothes that have pictures of things like snakes or severed eyeballs screened on them, and seem to be more in costume than in school clothes.

Many headbangers are into getting loaded and a number of them know very little about basic hygiene—although it may be part of the shock treatment to walk around with greasy hair and teeth that will need a chisel to remove the plaque on them.

Party Animals

Even in middle school you may find these creatures. They live to party . . . which usually means drinking booze until they throw up or doing various kinds of drugs.

Much of what party animals talk about is pure fiction,

but some of them really do have access to drinks and drugs through older friends, brothers and sisters, and sometimes even their parents. Needless to say, it's a bad idea to hang out with this crowd, even though the kids in it seem carefree and fun-loving. The fire they are playing with is deadly.

Fashion Models

These girls spend all of their time leafing through fashion magazines, going to the malls to try on endless outfits, and putting on makeup. They begin shaving their legs before they have hair on them and spend their entire allowances on hair products. Some of them even refuse to suit up for gym class because they are afraid of messing up their hair.

Except for the fact that their bodies are undeveloped, these girls dress and look a lot older than they really are. Unfortunately, the ability to look older doesn't make a person more mature. Still, they put on a good act.

The male version of this species is rare in middle school, but is often found in high school. They are called "*G.Q.*ers" after a fashion magazine created for men. You'll find them under the "best dressed" section in the school yearbook.

Burnouts

Burnouts are the kids who have really had to struggle to make it as far as sixth grade. They show up for school when the wind blows them in the right direction and seem to come from homes where no one knows who they are.

Burnouts never do their homework, have lost their school books, and are just putting in time until they can flunk out of school completely. Many burnouts have been to "juvy" (juvenile hall) as more than visitors. They often cloud the bathroom with smoke and refuse to suit up for P.E.

Clowns

Although this species does not technically group together, these individuals are found in every class or group. Clowns often can be persuaded to do things that normal people would never do: wash their hair in toilets, spill marbles in the hall during class break, eat bugs . . . anything, as long as it gets them some laughs.

Clowns are fun to have around as long as they know when to quit, a skill they usually lack.

Brains

You probably know who fits into this category. Yep! It's those kids born with IBM computers for brains. Really smart kids often hang out together, either because no other group wants them around or because no one else has a vocabulary large enough to understand them. The funny thing is that most average kids distance themselves from the brain group just until they need help on the big quiz in English.

Sex Fiends

This strange kid is a subspecies of various species. Almost always boys, sex fiends talk or joke about sex, body parts, and girls endlessly. A giant walking hormone, this kind of boy rarely has a real girlfriend. Instead, he spends his spare time drooling over the pages of "naked lady" magazines and other pornography.

His fascination with sex causes him to limit his friendships to those who don't mind a constant bombardment of sexual talk. What this kid really needs is to get involved in an active sport and take an ice cold shower.

Floaters

Most likely, you'll start middle school as a floater. Floaters don't really have to identify with a particular group. Instead they move freely between groups. Floaters generally feel a little bit left out because they are not firm members of any species on campus. At the same time, most floaters are happy to have the large number of acquaintances and friends that moving between groups offers.

The Unclean

Remember reading in the Bible about the people who

contracted leprosy and had to stay away from the general population for fear they would give others the disease? Well, there usually are a few kids on campus who fit into this outcast category.

Most of the time, these kids do not band together as a group but rather remain lonely and friendless.

The reasons for their sad plight are numerous. Sometimes it's because they look, smell, or dress oddly, and sometimes it's because of all three. Sometimes they have poor social skills and find it hard to make friends. Most of the time there is little an outcast can do to break into a group. Instead, they become the target of all of those cowardly enough to make jokes at their expense.

Bloods, Homeboys, and Honkeys

In some schools you will find that certain kids hang out with other kids of a similar race or culture. Sometimes these groups dress in a particular way or listen to a certain kind of music. Often, among themselves, they will make rude racial jokes or comments about others who are not like them.

Naturally this kind of grouping does very little to help ease tension and hostility. These kids come off real strong and pushy . . . as long as they have their gangs to back them up. Transfer these guys to schools where they cannot hang out with others of their race or culture and they become timid in a hurry.

Choosing Your Group

In your middle school you can probably identify a number of species that I haven't even mentioned in this chapter. The important thing to remember is to be wise in picking the species you want to hang out with and to avoid thinking that your group is so much better than any other.

When it comes time to pick or locate the group you want to hang out with, follow a few tips:

Hang out with winners and you'll become a winner; hang out with losers and you'll become a loser. In other words, take a long, hard look at the people in the group that you would like to be a part of. Make sure that these people are the kind of people that you really want to be like. Make sure that they are not into doing things that you know are wrong or unhealthy for you physically or spiritually.

You will tend to become like those you spend time with. This can have a great effect on what you are going to become in the future. For example, if you struggle a bit getting decent grades, it would be real dumb (although admittedly comfortable) to hang out with people who ditch classes or do poorly in school. These friends won't build you up; they will bring you down to their level. In contrast, if you hang out with people who do well in school, you will find that your grades improve as well.

Don't join any old group that will accept you. You don't need to be desperate. Some groups will take anyone who does what is required by the group. Be selective enough to hang out with the kind of people you really like and don't have to be ashamed of.

Be careful about putting down other groups or species on campus. This kind of behavior may be fun (laughing at someone else's strangeness usually is), but it leads to a snotty attitude and a very nasty condition called "false pride."

One Last Word

Finding a good group of friends to hang out with can be one of the best experiences in middle school. Finding the wrong species of friends to hook up with can also be one of the worst turning points in your life. Be wise.

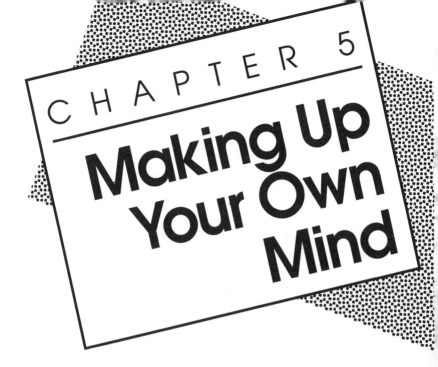

CHAPTER 5

Making Up Your Own Mind

Answer these questions honestly: How would you feel if your mom selected your school clothes for you each day? Or if your friends cancelled your order at the golden arches and ordered what *they* wanted you to eat instead? Or if someone told you what music to listen to and what music is junk?

I think I know what you would feel and say: "I can make up my own mind!" And you would very likely be right. Unless you're color blind, can't read a menu, or have X-rated taste in music, you probably are able to make these decisions for yourself. You've come to a point in life at which you will have to make up your own mind about things. Not only about what to wear to school, what to eat, and what to listen to, but also about many other important issues in life.

Peer Pressure

The most frequent response I hear when the subject of peer pressure comes up is, "I don't let anybody tell me what to do. I make my own decisions!" Maybe so. But living in this world, it's far more likely that we will find ourselves bending with the influences of society and especially our friends.

During a recent experiment,[2] a group of students was placed in a room with a projector and a huge screen. On the screen was an image of three numbered lines, two of similar length and one obviously of greater length. The researchers gave the group a moment to study the lines, turned off the projector, and asked the individuals in the group to identify which line had been the longest.

Sounds easy, huh? Well, there was a catch. All of the

participants except one had been privately instructed to select the line that was not the shortest but obviously was also not the longest. When the researchers asked the group to give their choices, all except the unknowing participant voted for the *wrong* line. Seeing that he was outnumbered by the group, the individual who *knew* the right answer, changed his mind, decided that he was mistaken, and voted for the wrong answer.

The researchers conducted the experiment a number of times with different groups. On each occasion, the student who actually knew the right answer voted with the majority, anyway. This is an example of classic peer pressure: to go against what you know to be true and right in order to be in step with the rest of the group.

Critical Choices

Of course it makes little difference if we go along with the crowd decision on the length of a line, but it makes a whole world of difference if we go along with them on other things, like hurting other people or going against our own convictions.

One of the first things you must understand when you start making your own decisions is that people are prone to become clones. In other words, your friends and society mold you a whole lot more than you realize. Think about it. Do you like the same style of music your friends like? Do you favor the same sports or activities? Do you dress in the same style? Do you use the same slang phrases, tell the same jokes, use the same words? "Well sure," you say, "but having these things in common is what made us friends." That's possible, but it's more likely that because you are friends, you have become alike.

You can see this process at work on your school campus. Imagine that a kid starts hanging out with some guys who speak pig latin, shave polka dots out of their hair, and howl at the moon. It'll be just a matter of time before this normal kid becomes a moon-howling, polka-dot-headed, pig-latin-chirping member of the tribe.

Be Choosy

Because our friends influence us, we must try to pick quality people for our friends. In the experiment I just shared with you, when the researchers tried the routine with *two* suckers instead of one, the pair banded together and insisted that they were right and everyone else was wrong. And of course, they were correct. The Bible advises, "Bad company corrupts good character" (1 Corinthians 15:33).

It is important to acknowledge that we *do* want to be like our friends. We don't want to be outcasts. We're afraid that if we resist the flow of the group too much we will be kicked out of the club. The independence we claim so proudly often goes only as far as our group allows.

Some people will go to almost any length to be part of the crowd. Jeff, a kid in my youth group, is one of those guys—a nice kid, but a wannabe follower of whatever group would accept him. He had a wishbone for a backbone.

On a warm summer afternoon, Jeff and a few of his friends took to the back roads of their small town. Quite suddenly, they came upon the carcass of a large toad. Now this toad had been dead for a number of days and had been flattened into a frisbee by passing cars. It was in lousy shape.

After a number of gross jokes, someone in the group dared Jeff to eat the toad. When Jeff balked, the pressure increased. Accusations of cowardice were added, and triple-dog-dare-ya's were heaved onto the pile. Finally, the demands to eat the toad were reduced to merely taking a bite out of it. Jeff reached down, picked up the dried toad, and bit off his crispy little head, immediately spitting it into the bushes. The group howled in laughter and groaned in disgust. Soon Jeff's actions were legendary. He was offered the honor of being the school geek. (In case you don't know, the definition of a geek is "one who bites off the heads of animals in public.")

Jeff wanted to please his friends so much that he did the unthinkable to win their approval. Although most of us would stop short of chomping on dead toads to avoid being outcasts, we may be willing to do a whole bundle of other things. To understand and acknowledge this tendency is the first step towards truly being able to make up our own minds.

In a middle school setting you will probably have the opportunity to see, hear, and do a lot of things that would never have been part of your elementary school experience. Swings and sandboxes are out. Being cool is in. Some of these ideas and activities will have to do with the things your friends enjoy. Some of the ideas and activities will be passed along through the school and through the teachers themselves. For every bit of information you receive, for every action you are invited to take part in, you will be expected to make up your own mind . . . or have someone else make it up for you.

Healthy Doubting

You may already have figured out that not everything you read, see, or hear—even from adults—is true or accurate. I remember when this truth first dawned on my son. We were standing in line at the supermarket, waiting to unload the piles of food quickly defrosting in our cart. Surrounding us at the check stand were goodies, begging for a chance to come home with us. Included were a number of so-called newspapers with names like *The National Snoop* and *The Daily Tattletale*.

One of these tabloids caught my son's attention. The headline declared, "Baby from Mars Born to a Human Mother," and nearby was a picture of a baby with small antennae protruding from its head. "Dad," he said in a serious tone, "a lady had a baby from Mars."

It was at this point that we had one of those long, father-to-son talks about not believing everything you see in print. The concept stunned him. "But how can they print it if it's not true?" he complained. Good question, but beside the point.

If we think for a few minutes, we will be able to see through the idiotic attempts people make to get us to believe that the products they sell will create magic. Take, for example, a mouthwash that promises to give its users sex appeal. Imagine a big, green-toothed, greasy-haired, rumpled, wart-faced junk collector. Do you imagine for one second that giving this guy a swig of this miraculous mouthwash will suddenly cause him to be overrun with beautiful girls in bikinis? Not a chance.

Ads like this are created and aired for one reason: because they work. There are a whole lot of mental midgets sitting in front of TV screens who figure that if something is said over the airwaves, it must be true.

Get Picky

In middle school you will be doing a whole lot of picking. You will be picking your friends, your clothes, your music, your sports, your image, and sometimes even your nose (hopefully not in public). You will be making choices. It's an awesome responsibility.

Sometimes you will make the wrong choice. For example, let's suppose that you decide to hang out with Jenny Brown. You think she is nice, friendly, and funny. Some of your other friends think she is a creep; your mom dislikes her so much that she wants you to wear a garlic wreath and crucifix around your neck and keep a hammer and wooden stake handy.

The reactions of your mom and friends only push you further into the friendship. You find yourself defending Jenny, even when you have second thoughts about the friendship yourself. As time goes by, you find that every time Jenny visits your house, some of your clothes go home with her—*without your permission*. Naturally, Jenny either denies that she has taken anything or claims that you said she could borrow the item.

Slowly you come to discover that Jenny is not quite the person you thought she was. She has morals and habits that would get you put under house arrest until you are eighteen if you imitated them. Jenny is not the kind of friend that you had hoped she would be. You've made a mistake in judgment, and your mom—in one of her rare moments—was right after all. So you go looking for a wooden stake.

One Last Word

It is very important that you make up your own mind about your relationship with God. If you were raised in a

Christian home, it's possible that as a child you merely adopted the values and ideas of your family. Now it's time for you to decide if you truly want to know and walk with God. You can't inherit Christianity genetically like you inherit brown eyes, curly hair, buck teeth, or a beak nose.

Christianity is a *choice*. Your upbringing can help you see the choice more clearly, but it cannot choose for you.

You'll have to do some hard thinking about what it really means to be a follower of Christ. Not everyone is willing to do what it takes to be a true believer. If you have questions or doubts about God or about the Bible, talk to a Christian adult whom you trust. You'll be able to get helpful information that will allow you to make an intelligent choice.

To make up your mind in favor of a relationship with God does not mean that you are going to be perfect. It often means failure. But it is the same kind of failure that you experienced as a baby when you were learning to walk. You didn't give up—you don't now crawl to school! Nope, you whipped up a little more determination and pulled yourself up for another try. True faith is very much like that. In the end, your faith will have to be your own and not anyone else's. It's up to you to make up your mind.

CHAPTER 6

Love and Romance— Middle School Style

Some of you may want to skip this chapter. The members of the opposite sex are of no interest to you. In fact, you and your buddies have made a pact promising *never* to like girls. Or maybe you are simply too busy having fun to take notice of the whole boyfriend/girlfriend scene.

No problem! Just come back and read this chapter when ol' Cupid decides to stick you with one of his arrows. You have plenty of time to deal with the subject at hand. Enjoy what interests you now. But the rest of you, please consider some of these thoughts.

Secret Loves

The vast majority of middle school romances are one-sided. In other words, one person really likes another person but never ever tells them so or ever manages to get the other person to like them back. The person who is "in love" often hopes that the other person will notice them and start to like them in return, but the relationship rarely works out.

This is a tough situation for the kid who really wishes to win the affection of a secret love, but most people in

this situation choose to keep quiet rather than risk rejection. What I'm trying to tell you is that if you get all the way through middle school without ever really having a true girlfriend or boyfriend, don't worry! You are the average person, not the weirdo.

For those of you who are brave enough to try communicating your interest in another person, you will face the problem of how to do so. The usual method is to tell your big-mouthed friends and then sit back and wait for them to spread the news. And believe me, they will! They'll probably go right up to the guy you like and say something direct like, "Hey, did you know that Jennifer likes you?"

You can also try calling him or her on the phone. This can be very scary. After all, what do you say? You have to have a reason to call—at least the first time. And what if the person you call is really cold on the other end of the phone? What if you get their parents?

When phone calls are not an option, I have seen some brave (or desperate) people write love notes. Never, *ever* write down anything you don't want the whole world to hear about. For certain, somebody will help your love scribbles get the circulation they *don't* deserve. You'll show your love note to some friends, and they, being such good friends, will steal it, photocopy it, and pass it around the school. Another awful thing that can happen is that your mom or dad will discover the love note. So—if you *must* write a love note, use disappearing ink on self-destructing paper.

The Bad News

Once two people in middle school discover each other—and like I said, this is not really the average situation—they are faced with a whole bunch of other things to consider. Most kids in middle school are not allowed to date (I am defining a *date* as going somewhere alone with your boyfriend or girlfriend). So the couple ends up hanging out together at school, during games, or at church events.

Some of them want to be alone so bad they cram themselves into the "make-out row" in the back of the van or bus, the back rows of the movie theater, or any deep, dark woods they can find. This desire to want to hang out with the person you like so much is very natural . . . but it may also cause some problems with your friends.

Kids who get overly involved in romantic relationships will lose ground with their other friends. Their pals will no longer bother to invite them to play football because "lover boy" is too busy with his girlfriend—or even worse, wants to drag her along everywhere. (And besides, most of Romeo's friends don't have girlfriends, so they are extremely unsympathetic). The girls may be a little more faithful to a friend skewered by Cupid's arrow, but they become jealous eventually and grow tired of hearing about how great so-and-so is. Having a boyfriend or girl-friend is the pits for your other social life!

Most middle school romances have short life ex-pectancies. It's rare to find people who have been togeth-er for more than six months. Most of the time kids just get bored or a new prospect comes along.

A lot of people who have partners in middle school do something called *going together*. This simply means that they are not interested in getting new boyfriends or girlfriends right now . . . give them a month or two. Some kids get really emotional about going together and exchange rings or necklaces. Things can get very gooey.

Parents' Reactions

By the way, parents react to the news that their children are going steady in different ways. Some go crazy, threatening to shoot their daughter's boyfriend if he comes around; others smile and say, "That's nice," or "Isn't it cute? Junior has found himself a little girlfriend!" Besides making you want to puke, this kind of parental sputter can make you feel sort of dumb and childish. A few parents will want to lock their kids in the house until they are eighteen. It's not really your parents' fault that they act this way. They just never expected you to get serious about someone of the opposite sex until you were almost ready to be married. They don't know how to react!

Phone Trouble

People who like each other often find themselves talking on the phone a lot . . . and I mean *a lot*! This can be incredibly boring. I know plenty of kids who run out of things to say and end up just listening to the person breathe. One kid in our youth group actually fell asleep with the phone to her ear while listening to her boyfriend sleep.

If you start spending a lot of time talking on the phone, expect your parents to flip out. They will undoubtedly give you a telephone time limit or make you pay for your own phone line. Or they may cut off your tongue. This is fair since the phone in an average house has to be shared by the entire family. And your dad may not agree that a call from "Bubba" is as important as the call he is expecting from his boss.

A word of advice might be helpful to those of you who find yourself wanting to spend hours talking to your boyfriend or girlfriend: Some people don't really like to talk on the phone. (If *you* are one of these people, make sure you tell your boyfriend or girlfriend right away.) Be careful not to make your friend feel obligated to call you. Once people start to feel obligated and are expected to do certain things, they often start feeling trapped and want out of the relationship.

A long time ago, only desperate girls called boys. Although times have changed, there is still a bit of wisdom in letting boys do the telephone calling. My reasoning is simple. If a boy thinks he is pursuing you, he will tend to stay interested. (Right, guys?) We seem to find what is just out of our grasp very appealing. If a boy thinks he is being chased . . . well, he may use you for a little while, but he won't really like being chased for very long. In other words, a wise girl doesn't call a boy she likes—no matter how much she wants to—unless she is invited to.

Broken Hearts

If you are having a serious boyfriend/girlfriend relationship think carefully about what I am going to tell you next. Expect to be dumped. It happens to almost everyone sooner or later, and to some of us a whole bunch of times. Being dumped really hurts, especially if you still have feelings for the person who dumped you. You will feel rejected, crushed, angry, and even stupid for liking the person who hurt you.

Although getting dumped can be terribly painful, the pain won't kill you. You'll live and probably even find

yourself attracted to someone else in a short time. Most of your friends will try to comfort you by telling you what a moron your old girlfriend or boyfriend was and by reminding you that there are "other fish in the sea." But such pearls of wisdom aren't always enough to comfort broken hearts.

After a breakup, expect your relationship with that other person to be a little bit weird. In fact, it may be very, *very* weird. What I mean is that most people find that it's hard to go back to being just friends after having a romantic relationship. This is especially true if you have become physically involved. Your former boyfriend or girlfriend will probably avoid you, stop hanging out with you or your group, and possibly say some pretty harsh things about you. As you may find out, there is a price you pay for a relationship.

Sex

Even though most kids in middle school don't have full-blown passionate romances, there are always a few who do. Sometimes a girl is hounded by older boys, and sometimes kids from your own peer group find themselves playing kissy face. If you find yourself in this category, pay special attention to the rest of this chapter, because we are going to talk about sex. Kids in middle school often have tons of questions about sex and dating. Most of them are too shy or embarrassed to ask those questions. Although I don't want to make this book into a manual on sex, I would like to give you some tips that will help you keep this area of your life from smacking into trouble. If you have questions that I don't answer, please, talk to an adult you can trust. She or he may get embarrassed, too, but will probably try to answer your questions.

Sex begins whenever you get physical with another person. *Having sex* means the act of intercourse. *Sexuality* in a relationship starts when your body takes hold of someone else's. Some kids start to play with sex while still in middle school, but like playing with fire, a few who are not careful end up getting burned.

Sex is a good thing. It is a gift from God. He created it, designed all the parts and pieces, and installed the engine that drives it. But he also put conditions on it for our own good and for the good of those around us. For example, imagine that you have been given a car that is a drag racer. There is a time and place to use a drag racer and a time and place *not* to use one. The proper place is on a drag strip; the improper place is on the streets downtown. Using your drag racer to get to McDonald's will endanger your life and the lives of others. Drag racers are made for a special purpose.

Sex is a bit like a drag racer. You can start its engines and sit behind the wheel, but once you back it onto the neighborhood street, you're asking for trouble. Sex is an

act meant for marriage, just as the drag racer is meant for a drag strip. Let me speak frankly: Despite what you see on TV or in the movies, despite what friends, parents, or relatives may do or say, having sex before a life commitment to another person (marriage) is wrong in God's eyes.

Danger Zones

You might want to keep a few things in mind if you end up playing around with sex. First of all, expect anything you do physically with your boyfriend (or even girlfriend) to be told around the school. This isn't very nice, but it's the way things are. Some boys like to brag about how far they got with their girlfriends, which is a creepy thing to do. Kids like to talk and spread rumors. And it will be doubly true after you break up. You are giving others ammunition when you have sex with someone.

If you make out with lots of people, you'll get a bad reputation. If you are a girl, you may find boys try to pick up on you. They'll want to mess around with you because they will think that they can get you to play around sexually without too much effort. If you are a boy, girls will think you are insincere and have a one-track mind—a dirt track.

Sex is like going downhill on a bicycle. You get lots of sensation, you pick up speed and distance as you go, but putting on the brakes becomes harder and harder. And as you may know from experience, the faster you go on a bike, the nastier the results are if you crash. The same is true with sex. If you get yourself into a situation where you are having sex or even coming close to having it, you may find a big surprise awaits you down the road.

Many kids who want to do the right thing have asked me, "How far should you go in playing around with sex?" The best advice I can give is to keep private things private. In other words, if you consider a part of your body private and personal, keep it that way and don't share it with others.

Don't buy dumb lines like: "If you love me, you'll let me," "What's the matter? Are you a prude?" and "Why not? Everyone else does." These are old tricks used by insincere people to get their way. The funny thing is that although these tricks are ancient, people still fall for them.

Make it easy on yourself—avoid sexual temptations. Think about it—if you knew the neighbor's pit bull was hungry, would you hang over the fence eating a steak sandwich? If the dog took part of your hand along with your meal, most people would say that you asked for it.

One Last Word

Sexual desire is like a hungry dog. Keep temptation out of reach. For example, don't fill your head with garbage from sex magazines, steamy movies, or videos. This kind of stuff is easy to find and plenty of guys look at it. But it won't help you keep your mind off sex.

If you have a boyfriend or girlfriend, avoid situations in which you can get physical without being discovered.

Don't invite your boyfriend over while you are baby-sitting. Not only is this dumb, but you can also expect the little kids to squeal if they catch you. And don't have the person you adore come to your house when you know you'll be alone. This kind of setup will make it very difficult to put the brakes on sex.

Love and romance "middle school style" can be fun and exciting if you are wise in the way that you handle them.

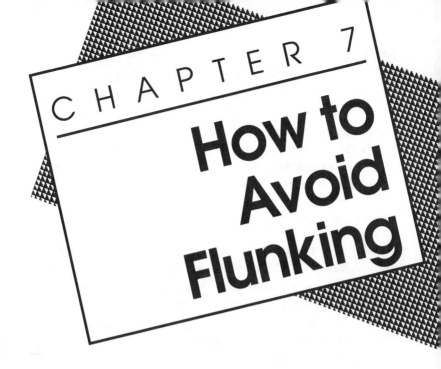

CHAPTER 7

How to Avoid Flunking

t may not surprise you that many kids who get pretty good grades in elementary school end up with dismal results their first year in middle school. The main reason for this drop is that kids are getting used to a new system: multiple teachers with varying demands, an increased homework load, and loads of distractions.

In this chapter I'd like to give you a few tips on how to keep your grades from sliding into the basement. Most of the stuff I'm telling you is pure common sense. If you get a grasp on them now, they will serve you the rest of your school life and possibly far beyond.

Be Positive

You'll notice every kind of attitude in every class, from kids who are present in body only to kids who are trying to get passing grades out of fear they will be beaten with nail-studded bats if they don't. Attitudes are funny things: If you expect to get rotten grades in school, guess what—you probably will! And if you set your mind on getting good grades, you usually will get them, too. The struggle of learning is not so much a matter of skill as it is a matter of attitude. Skill in a subject can be learned, but attitudes come from within.

Be Prepared

Come to class every day with everything you need to do the business at hand. For example, make sure you have your books, a notebook filled with paper, sharpened pencils with erasers not yet chewed off, a pen, and whatever else is required for the class. Try to avoid being one of those people who always tries to bum a pencil or a piece of paper off of a neighbor.

Be Organized

Once you have your class goodies, it's helpful to get them organized. Just before school starts each year, almost every store carries those cool, glow-in-the-dark notebooks that have dividers for each class; a place to stash pencils; a built-in calculator; handy charts that will allow you to convert any measurement into metric, bells, or whistles; a place for pictures of your dog; the constitution translated into fourteen languages; and an emergency life raft. With a tool like this one, you can organize your life with very little effort.

Most students *start* school organized. But by the second week or so, things begin to deteriorate. By keeping your school stuff neat, you'll be able to find what you need when you need it. And being neat will keep you from losing or damaging important papers. Papers are more impressive if they aren't dog-eared or streaked with today's lunch. Neatness takes time, but in the end it saves lots of time—time that you otherwise have to spend looking for lost papers or assignments.

Catch the System

In each of your classes, your teacher will have requirements that you will have to fill in order to get a decent grade. This way of doing things is called the class's *system*. Some classes are a breeze! All you have to do is to show up with a pencil and you get a good grade. Other classes are much tougher. You've already experienced systems to some degree in elementary school. Then you only had to get used to one or two teachers' systems; now, you have to figure out five or six systems.

In order to keep track of what is required for each class, pay close attention, especially for the first several weeks. Write down everything your teachers tell you to do in a notebook. Some kids use special little notebooks to keep track of their assignments.

Avoid Goof-Offs

If at all possible, avoid sitting around people who will keep you from getting your work done in class. If you

have friends who try to talk to you or if you sit between two guys who carry on daily spit-wad wars, see if you can move to another seat. If you *really* want to position yourself to concentrate in class, sit right up front. It will keep you on your toes. The only drawback to sitting up front that *I* can think of is if your teacher sprays when he or she talks. . . .

Suit Up

To avoid doing poorly in P.E., follow one simple rule: Suit up and play. A few kids never suit up. Some of them think they are too cool to play organized sports. Some are afraid of the ball or of sweat. Some of them consistently forget their gym clothes at home. The typical coach does not take nonsuits lightly. Your grades will be affected if you fail to suit up and play.

Sometimes a teacher will lower your P.E. grade if you forget to take your gym suit home and wash it. Here's a rule of thumb: If your socks can stand up by themselves, they are overdue for a wash. Most kids take their P.E. clothes home on Fridays, which means that bus trips home on that day are the smelliest of the week!

Do Your Homework

Even though it seems very unfair to have to go to school all day long and then get stuck with more work on top of that, homework is a sad fact of life. Most teachers are very serious when they say that homework projects must be completed, so get used to them. I realize some elementary schools give out a little homework, but nothing like what you'll be assigned in middle school.

Since you're going to be stuck with homework, make the best of it. If you can develop a few good habits and a little discipline, you'll be able to get your homework done quickly and still maintain its quality. The following tips will help make homework as painless as possible:

Find the right place. Don't try to do homework in a place where you are going to be bothered by little sisters eating your papers or your folks tripping over you. Find yourself a desk or table with some good lighting far away from the rest of the family and do your homework there. And sit up! The kids who try to finish their homework as they lie on their beds usually end up falling asleep with their noses in their textbooks.

Some people try to do their homework while watching TV, listening to the stereo, or talking on the phone. This makes working a little difficult. The fewer interruptions and distractions you have, the faster you'll finish your work and be free to do what you really want to do with your afternoon or evening.

In giving you this advice, I realize that what might distract one person is background noise to another. Use common sense as you decide what kinds of conditions you can really work under and what kinds will keep you from getting on with the job.

Avoid snacking. This bit of wisdom comes from the

common experience of having just completed a lengthy homework assignment and knocking a glass of milk all over it. And most teachers don't like to receive papers with gooey bits of pizza still stuck to them. Give yourself a break and eat in the kitchen. You'll be glad that you did!

Do it now. This goes for finishing homework, studying for tests, and working on any other projects that must be done by a deadline. There is nothing worse than feeling panic swell up inside as you realize that you have one night left to complete a science notebook that you should have been working on all month.

Even though it's a drag, work on your projects *before* they hit anxiety level. Save yourself the stress and probable failure by getting these kinds of jobs done before a course is over. This may mean practicing "delayed gratification" and refusing to do what you want to do right when you want to do it. But putting off pleasures for the moment will make you enjoy them even more when the work at hand is completed.

The same lecture on delayed gratification fits here, too: Do your weekend work on Friday night rather than on

Sunday night and you'll find that the weekend is a whole lot more enjoyable because no assignments hang over your head.

Work in blocks. Working under self-imposed pressure can increase the quality of your study time. Give yourself a certain time period within which to complete a task. Refuse to quit or take a snack break until that block of time is used up or the job is finished, whichever comes first.

Develop work integrity. Sometimes it will be tempting to let a friend, an older brother or sister, or even one of your parents do your homework for you—or at least give you all of the answers. This may get your work done quickly, but it will hurt you in the long run.

Make no excuses. It's funny how often people with unfinished homework assignments blame it on some disaster. I can assure you that your teacher has already heard all the sad-eyed stories about homework-eating dogs, paper-snatching tornadoes, and notebook-snatching thieves. Don't even bother telling them. You'll just make yourself look stupid.

Cheaters Never Win

Once you get the homework habit down, there's one more little thing that you need to think about. That little thing is the subject of cheating. Some people spend more time figuring out clever ways to cheat on class exams than they would have spent studying for them. You've probably seen many of their sneaky devices: cheat sheets written on thin paper and shoved up sleeves, answers written on hands or forearms in ink, or (my favorite) carefully created answer sheets placed in the chambers of clear pens.

Most teachers have seen all of these tricks . . . many times. If you are busted for cheating, not only will your grade suffer, but you will also heap shame on yourself and—if you are a Christian—on the reality of your faith.

You see, cheating is stealing and deception. If you get your answers off someone else's paper, you are stealing that work. If you get your answers from a cheat sheet, you are lying to your teacher about what you know. You'd think that kids who claim to be Christians would know that cheating is wrong and would never do so. But you and I know that the temptation to cheat is so strong that some kids give in to it over and over again.

Difficult Classes

If you are really trying to do your best in a class and still get poor grades, you may be in a class that is too advanced for you. Perhaps you have not yet mastered the foundational material that you must know to make it in the class.

One seventh-grade student I know was only an average math student but was somehow dropped into the most advanced math class his school offered. Try as he could, the best grade he could manage was a D. The school kept him in the class for an entire year. In the meantime, he fell further and further behind, lost in a cloud of confusion and frustration. Somebody in the scheduling office had goofed.

The next year he transferred down a notch into a class almost as advanced as his last one and still far beyond his limits. But by this point, it no longer mattered. He had given up on math and had developed a strong distaste for the subject.

If you think this is happening to you, go straight to your counselor and ask to be transferred into an easier class. And don't be ashamed to do so. A simple schedule change can make a big difference.

One Last Word

Although getting good grades comes easier to some than others, most of us can get pretty good grades with a combination of common sense and a bit of personal discipline. This effort is good practice for the adult world. Kids who always look for easy ways out often play now and pay later. I hope they enjoy working in car washes for the rest of their lives.

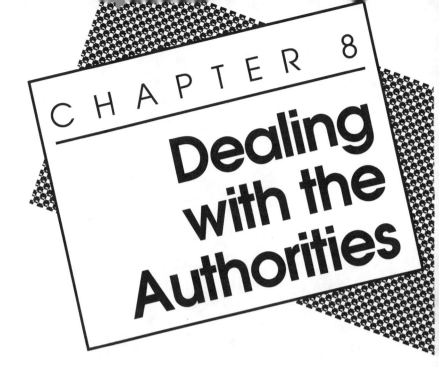

CHAPTER 8

Dealing with the Authorities

Have you ever noticed that in old Westerns you can tell the good guys from the bad guys by the hats they wear? Good guys wear white hats and have shiny white teeth; bad guys wear black hats, need a good shave, and have black goo covering their pearlies.

Come to think of it, you can figure out almost everybody's role by looking at his or her hat: old ladies wear funny bonnets, stuffy town-folk wear derby hats, the undertaker wears a crumpled top hat, and the beautiful damsel wears no hat at all. Before the actors in these old films even speak a line or sing a love song to a cow on the prairie, you understand their roles in the drama, thanks to the hats they wear.

As you go through life in middle school, you'll find yourself meeting a lot of people who are wearing different hats. They are the "authorities" in charge of you. Each one has a role to play in the day-to-day drama of middle school . . . and it may surprise you to discover that some of these people intentionally put on black hats.

Let's check out the various authorities you will bump up against as you travel through middle school and then consider some tips that can keep that trip from becoming unpleasant.

School Authorities

I'm sure that you assume that every adult in your school is an authority. This may be true, but there are various levels of authority. The school janitor is an authority, but has nowhere near the power of a vice principal. So who are your school authorities and what do they do?

The Principal

The principal is the boss of the school. He wears a white hat. He wants to make you happy, your parents happy, the teachers happy, and his bosses at school district central happy. Most school principals don't get too involved in the everyday lives of average students. They present the blue ribbons, give the speeches, handle big, big problems, and do lots of paperwork. You will probably see the principal around but rarely will you be called into his or her office . . . except by mistake. If you go to a small school, you'll be more likely to see and talk to the principal. If you go to a large school, you may only see the principal on special occasions.

The Vice Principal

The vice principal usually wears a black hat. In big schools there may be several vice principals. If you get called into the vice principal's office, start sweating bullets, because the V.P. handles the real nasty jobs at school. They deal with the guys who blow up toilets or get into fights. They deal with troublemakers, chronic truants, and those caught selling school secrets to terrorists. They have the power to kick you out of school, make you do grounds cleanup, or—worst of all—call your parents. Mind your manners when the V.P. comes around.

Some V.P.'s are actually very nice people who have taken on a job that is guaranteed to make them unpopular. Other V.P.'s take the job because they can't find steady work as professional torturers anywhere else.

School Secretaries

Many schools have a battalion of people who make it their job to keep attendance records, handle paperwork, and keep you from seeing your counselor if you are without an ap-

pointment. Most of them have seen every trick in the book. They can tell when you have tried to duplicate one of your parent's signatures on an excuse note. Probably, they are the true brains behind your school.

Counselors

Most schools assign you to an adult who is to be your guiding angel through middle school. This person is your counselor. If you do a lousy job of keeping your grades up, chances are you will end up in the counselor's office.

Counselors wear white hats. In the ten minutes that they have you in their offices, they want to become your pal. They are probably the ones who will contact your parents if you are bombing in your classes. They also handle minor discipline problems for vice principals. If you are caught chewing gum in class for a third time, you may find yourself sitting in the counselor's office for the rest of the class period rather than being stretched out on the torture rack in the V.P.'s office.

Campus Security

On some middle school campuses, you will discover one or two people wearing what look like police uniforms, complete with walkie-talkies and badges. At first glance you may wonder whether you have enrolled in school or are serving a prison sentence.

These are the security guards, also known as "rent-a-cops." Their job is to make sure undesirables from the community don't come around to hassle smaller kids like you and to be the campus cop. Unless you are doing terrible things (like littering) you will probably never be bothered by these guys.

Teachers

Teachers are the main authority figure you will face on a regular basis. They all have their own styles of discipline and control. Some will bust you for the slightest infraction of the rules while others walk around in a daze as the kids run amuck.

It is usually best to not get on a teacher's bad side right off the bat. This will work against you for the rest of the year. Just as you will develop an impression of each teacher during the first week of school, each teacher will also have a first impression of you. If you act up, fall asleep at your desk, come in late, or mouth off on the first day, your teacher will probably consider you in less than a positive light.

Even though teachers are supposed to deal with you in a neutral fashion, they are human and cannot help but give breaks to those they like . . . and drill to the wall those they don't. Like most authorities, teachers like to be right or superior in their judgments and do not take it very well if students put them in their place. I know about this fact from hard experience.

I once had a devout Mormon for an English teacher. During the course of a lecture, she made the comment: "Even the Bible teaches that black people are inferior." As a Christian I knew that this statement was absolute nonsense. I also knew that Mormons considered blacks unable to reach what they call the *priesthood* in their religion because of this teaching on racial inferiority. (By the way, this teaching has since been abandoned by the Mormon church.)

My hand shot up. "Excuse me, teacher, but could you tell me where in the Bible it says that?" The class hushed. Who was this brave soul challenging the deep and unending well of knowledge residing in this teacher?

She responded with irritation, "Well I could, but I don't have a Bible." The class shifted its view back to me. Had I been checked? Was this the end of the defiant one? Never!

Ever resourceful, I produced a Bible from under my chair and offered it to her. She thumbed through the book for a few minutes, reddened in the face, and mumbled, "I can't seem to find it right now, but I'm sure it's in there."

Being a dumb kid and sensing blood, I continued after my prey by giving a little speech that would be my undoing (academically) in the class. "Well, I really doubt that what you claim is in the Bible can actually be found there. I suggest that you not make claims about things this serious unless you can back them up with proof."

By now I knew the whole room was cheering (silently, of course). It was David and Goliath! The mouse that roared! The small, insignificant insect of a student single-handedly toppling the mighty authority of the classroom! Hooray!

I left the class feeling that I had scored big time. It was not until grades came out that I realized I was earning a return on my investment. I suffered with D's from the class for a semester. Finally, after asking for and receiving a transfer to another English class, I ended the year with B's. The moral? Buck authority if you must, but be willing to pay the consequences.

For the most part, though, you will find that your teachers are fair, caring, and eager to be accurate in what they teach.

Coaches

Although coaches *are* teachers, they are different from the other kinds you will meet. It's generally unwise to lip off to coaches, since they may use you as a rag to wipe off home plate. Even worse, they may tell you to run laps, which is fine if you are a gazelle, but a drag if you are an eleven-year-old kid.

Coaches are also the lucky teachers who get to wear shorts and T-shirts all day long as part of their jobs.

Subs

All of you have had substitute teachers before. These poor souls come willingly into classes that are without their regular teachers and try to keep the animals occupied.

Of course, as soon as the kids in a class hear that they are having a sub, they start making plans to switch seats and identities. Kids who try to pull these pranks naturally think that they are really creative and funny and that their sub is so dumb that she will never catch on. Actually, subs know all about this trick and *assume* that you are not whom you claim to be.

If subs wore hats, they would probably wear party hats, since most of the time they have you watch videos rather than do work.

Parents: The Final Authority

Of all the authorities in your middle school life, your parents are still the ones with major influence. Sometimes parents have a hard time when their kids go into middle school. They feel that they are losing the ability to direct and control the events in their kids' lives as they once did.

To add to this confusion, many middle school kids seek more and more independence from their parents. They want to be individuals and make their own decisions, decisions that may sometimes go against their parents' wishes.

As time goes on, you may find yourself getting into domestic squabbles with your parents. The rocky spots can have to do with just about anything: clothes you want to buy or wear, hairstyles, makeup, time spent on the phone, chores, grades, friends . . . you name it.

If you know what parents are looking for in your actions and attitude, it really can give you an advantage with this "prime authority" in your life. Most parents are very reasonable and will grant you more and more liberty if you show them that you are in control. Here are a few things that parents want to see in order before they are ready to give you the amount of leash you want.

Act responsibly. This is a big one for most parents. Parents need to see that you are not a flaky kid. This means you need to do your chores without being told. Clean up the messes you make without waiting for the "maid" to do it.

Do a good job on your chores or projects instead of trying to get by with the least amount of effort. For example, if it's your job to sweep the garage or driveway, move stuff and don't just sweep around it. Get in the corners and pick up the debris with a dustpan instead of blasting it into the neighbors' yard.

Responsibility means carrying your weight and not being a burden to somebody else. It means being on time or at the very least having the courtesy to call if there is some reason why you will be late. And responsibility is showing wisdom by avoiding bad situations or doing stupid things like shooting the pesky neighbor kid with your BB gun.

Communicate. Parents want to know what you are thinking and feeling. They need you to give them more than one-syllable responses to their questions. They really do need you to ask their advice from time to time and not just ask for more money.

Like everyone else, parents need to be told that they

are loved. Be sure to tell them often. Don't think that this shows weakness or is a corny thing to do.

Live a life your parents can be proud of. Would your folks be proud of you if they knew everything that you do? Make this your goal. If you find yourself hiding

things consistently and hoping your parents won't find out, it's a good bet that you are into some pretty sad stuff. It's also a good bet that God may not be too happy with how you are conducting your life, either.

Obedience. Obedience isn't always easy. But we need to listen to our parents and obey them even when we don't want to. When a kid starts to rebel, many parents just tighten the screws. When a kid obeys, they let up. It's that easy.

Some kids complain that if they did everything their parents asked them to do, they would end up with no life at all. This is rarely the case. Most parents simply need to see that you still know who's boss.

Show gratitude. A major gripe of most parents is that kids are ungrateful little creeps. From my perspective as a youth worker of many years, I have to say that this is a valid complaint. Kids rarely take the little bit of time it takes to tell their parents how much they appreciate what has been done for them. Just a few free words make all the difference in the world.

You see this in your own life. Suppose some friend keeps wanting you to feed her when she comes to your house. If this friend never said, "Thank you" when you rounded up a plate of goodies for her, but instead just dug right in, how would you feel? Or suppose a friend started needing you to loan him money or to buy him stuff when you went to the mall because he kept forgetting his money at home?

Imagine that the whole time this was going on, the most thanks you ever got was something mumbled under his or her breath. It wouldn't take long for you to feel used big time by this so-called friend. You never hear an expression of gratitude, merely of expectation.

Parents don't like feeling used, either. They give, not because it's expected, but because they love. You'll be miles ahead if you show them you are thankful!

One Last Word

Try out some of these tips. See if they don't help improve your life with the authority you can't transfer away from!

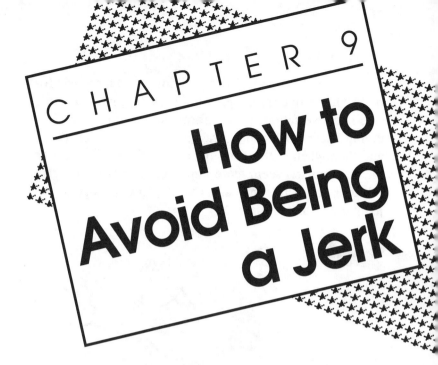

CHAPTER 9

How to Avoid Being a Jerk

I t's pretty safe to assume that no normal person wants to be thought of as a jerk. And it's pretty easy to avoid being one; you just have to avoid jerkish behavior! This chapter holds some hints about what you should do and avoid doing to keep from becoming a genuine jerk. Pay close attention, because once you earn the title of complete jerk, it's hard to get rid of. It's much better to avoid getting it in the first place.

Don't Brag

The fastest way to make people to dislike you is to try too hard to be liked and brag about yourself. It's okay to share real experiences or events in the context of an appropriate conversation. For example, if a bunch of kids are talking about scary things they have done, you can say, "Yeah, the time I tried sky-diving was the scariest for me!" This is not bragging, nor is it busting into someone else's conversation with information about your sky-diving accomplishments. Bragging is exaggeration (". . . and then when both of my parachutes failed, I. . . .") or making yourself seem more important than everyone else ("It took more guts than all of you've got put together to jump out of that airplane").

Most people are smart enough to know when to be impressed and when a story is being inflated with things that never really happened. It's not uncommon for kids who think they are being fed a load of manure by some braggart to challenge him or her to the test. "So . . . you can break bricks with your forehead, huh? Well, here's a pile of bricks. Let's see ya do it!" This means instant jerkdom for the poor slob whose imagination got the best of him or her during a story telling session. *Don't brag!*

Don't put on an act or try to be someone you are not. The skinny little kids smoking over in the corner may think they look mature and cool, but they fail to realize that almost everyone is laughing at them for trying to be someone other than themselves. You are not Rambo, a pro ball player, a movie star, or a fashion model, so don't try to act like one. Be who you really are.

Don't Blab

You may have had some experience with this truth already. In fact, your parents probably dropped this truth on you along with, "If you can't say anything nice, don't say anything at all." This shows that parents actually *are* right sometimes. It's wise advice to keep your mouth closed until you clear the content of your words with your brain.

If you are in trouble with the school bully, it may be because of something you said. If you make your best friend cry or hate you, no doubt it's because you said something thoughtless to her or about her. If you find yourself sitting on the toilet seat with a bar of Ivory soap bubbling in your mouth, it may be because you said that word without checking it through the proper filter and your dad happened around the corner at the same time. If you find yourself on your way to the office with a referral in your hand, it may very well be because you opened your big mouth in class when wisdom said to keep quiet and study.

Yep! Your mouth will get you into plenty of trouble, so weigh what you are going to say before you crank up your lips and start flapping.

This last word of advice is mainly for girls, since they are the ones who consistently pass notes or write long letters to each other. The stuff you send around class via person-to-person postal service is going to get read. This is fine if you don't have anything in your notes that is private. But if you record your personal feelings in your "Secret—Do not open upon threat of death" correspondence, it will be public knowledge by the end of the day.

Don't write down anything that you will feel dumb about if others read it. A home diary with a lock and key is where private thoughts should be kept.

Don't Lie

When a liar tells you something, do you believe it? Probably not. The problem with being or becoming a liar is that after a while people will not believe anything you say. Your word will be as valuable as play money. A friend once told me, "Your word is the most valuable thing that you have." People who cannot be trusted to tell the truth might as well be mute.

It's a terrible thing to be untrusted, to feel that the people you want to impress think you are a snake and what you say is not true. But it is a position into which we place ourselves by our actions. Liars are thought of as jerks. They have few friends. Even the members of their own families don't trust them. They usually don't even like themselves too well. So tell the truth, no matter how painful, ugly, and condemning it is. Facing the bitter consequences of truthfulness is always better than lying.

Don't Use People

If you win the lottery—I mean the big, *big* one—and everyone in school finds out about it, do you think that you will be treated differently? You bet! Boys and girls will want to borrow money with no intention of paying you back; friends will show up that you never knew existed. You will be a very popular person. But not because of who you are . . . because of your bucks!

Nobody likes to be used. We would hate it if some cute guy got to know us just in order to meet one of our friends. We would dislike it if our friends hung around with us just so they could swim in our pool, skate on our ramp, or jump on our trampoline. Yet it's so easy to use friends. People who are users or takers eventually find themselves friendless. Onetime friends now simply call them jerks.

Don't Mooch

Don't get in the habit of borrowing money or things from other people. If you *do* have to borrow something— which happens from time to time—return it or pay it back promptly.

The sad thing about most moochers is that they don't realize they are mooching. Even though they have a closet full of clothes that they borrowed from friends and have never returned, they think that because they *intend* to give the stuff back, they don't have a problem. Wrong!

Make it your goal to borrow as little as possible and always to return what you borrow.

Don't Victimize

In the jungle, the fit survive and the weak perish. In school some people act the same way. They find smaller, younger, frailer targets and then have fun at their expense. Since you are just coming into a new school situation, you probably can sense what life would be like if all the bigger kids decided to pick on you. It would be miserable!

Often people decide to pick on kids who look different, who are too fat, have big noses, different skin colors, or accents. Usually these kids cannot defend themselves and simply have to take the humiliation. Kids who tease in this way are first-class jerks—not to mention cowards.

You will find that kids in middle school have an incredible capacity for cruelty. Some sickos will torture animals; others delight in pestering classmates. The thing that all of these losers have in common is that they pick on those weaker than themselves in order to get a laugh.

On occasion a group of kids will act like piranhas and hassle an individual until he or she breaks into tears or fights back. Don't kick down a weaker person with your words or actions. The Bible warns that you may reap what you sow!

Don't Be Flaky

Flakes are people you can't count on. They are undependable, irresponsible, and careless. If your teacher assigns you to work in teams to create models of Egyptian pyramids, the flake of the group will never show up to work on the project outside of the classroom. And when they *are* in the classroom they won't contribute much to the project. But when grades are handed out, they will want to get A's for the project everyone else completed. This makes for very hard feelings toward the flakes involved.

One friend of mine had the misfortune to be assigned to a project with three flakes. None of them showed up to help her with the project, so she ended up doing the whole thing by herself. When she turned in the "group" project, she attached a note explaining that the other girls hadn't helped with the assignment and that it had been a solo effort.

My friend received an A in the class and her three flaky friends flunked. Boy, were they angry! (One thing you will notice about true jerks is that they get angry with others

for consequences that are their own fault.)

Flakes are people who refuse to take responsibility for their own actions or lack of action. They make excuses: "The dog ate my homework assignment"; "We ran out of Pampers and I had to use all my extra notebook paper to diaper my baby sister"; "There was an eclipse of the sun and I thought it was the end of the world, so I said to myself, 'No sense in doing my homework!' " Or they say dumb things like, "I forgot," "I couldn't find it," or "I didn't hear the instructions." Flakes *never* say, "I was lazy and irresponsible." No—they blame their failures on the actions of someone or something else. This is what makes them jerks as well as flakes.

Don't Be a Know-It-All

Sometimes you will come across kids who *have* to be right, even if they are completely wrong. They are stubborn, mule-headed, and unteachable. It's not a bad thing to be wrong, but it is a stupid thing to try to convince everyone you are right when it's clear you're not. It's all right to lose an argument. Changing your mind is not only permissible, but is sometimes also a good idea. You don't know and never will know everything. You don't have to. People will respect you for the things you do know. And they will respect you even more when you admit you've made a mistake or don't know something.

Even though everyone has an opinion, not everyone deserves to have one. I know very little about cars. I can drive them, fill them with gas, and change a tire, but other than that, I'm a complete idiot. During a discussion with some friends who happen to be good mechanics, opinions were exchanged about which brands of cars are good machines. When asked my thoughts on the subject, I honestly couldn't answer; I had to disqualify myself. Oh, I had an opinion and I could have offered that, but the sentiment would have been undeserved, because it would have been based on an ignorance of how cars work.

Keep your mouth shut if you are not really well informed about a subject.

Don't Cheat

I know that I've stressed this before, but none of us likes a cheater. We automatically think of people as jerks if they have to cheat to win. But as you know, cheating is a widespread habit and by the time you finish middle school, you will have seen lots of it.

Sometimes a kid who would never think of cheating in sports cheats like crazy in academic classes. A cheater is a cheater. Cheaters will do anything, even if it's wrong, for personal gain. A person who develops this trait becomes a loser for life.

One Last Word

Being a jerk is preventable. A bit of thoughtfulness and care, some self-control, and thought for the other person will keep you from ever wearing the title.

CHAPTER 10

You Need Friends

I met Tom in the seventh grade. We hung out in the same spot before school and our friendship grew out of that casual acquaintance.

Tom was never a dynamic personality at school—although he did receive temporary fame when he cut off half of his index finger with a table saw. For a week his misadventure was the talk of the lunch table. When he came back to school, the kids gathered round him to get their first glimpse of the bloody stump. Later he used the handicap to good advantage by inserting the stump into his nostril and pretending to pick all the way to his brain. Yep, a talented guy.

We continued to hang out through high school and during the summers of our college years, even though we went to schools in two different nations. Eventually we found ourselves working together in the same town and at the same company, and eventually even migrated to the same island in the Pacific.

Tom and I have had a friendship that is the kind you usually think of when you think of friends—a friendship that lasts forever, in which you live next door to each other (Tom and his family live a block away), mooch sugar from each other, goof off together, and laugh about old times. But in real life, this is a pretty rare situation. Most of your friends will come and go; most of your friendships will end when you graduate (or sooner), and you'll begin developing a whole new batch of friends.

In the next few pages, let's talk about developing two kinds of friendships. One kind you may experience during your time in middle school and, if you're fortunate, beyond. The other kind is even more important and, believe it or not, will last forever.

Everybody needs friends. Even loners who say that they would rather be alone need friends. It's a desire built into us by God. But not everyone knows how to make friends or, even more important, how to keep the friends they make.

Be Friendly

If you rarely talk, head straight for the corner when you're in a room full of people, or are so quiet that even your parents think that you're mute, making friends may be difficult. To make friends you must extend yourself, say, "Hi," and talk about subjects that are of common interest. The friendlier you are, the more friends you will make.

Be Loyal

A good friend doesn't act like a hummingbird, drinking nectar from your flower, and then flying off when a more attractive flower appears. True friends don't run off or change sides when other kids appear.

Being loyal does not mean that you become blind. A true friend will step in front of another who is heading into hurtful behavior. A real friend cares.

Be Genuine

True friends are never two-faced. They do not pretend to be good and trusted friends in order to hear all the deep dark secrets of another, and then blab them all around. If you are told something in confidence, keep it in confidence. I can only think of one exception: If a friend tells you about something that will harm her or him, like thoughts of suicide or that she or he uses drugs, confide those conversations to a responsible adult. But don't spread those confidences around school.

Be Well-Rounded

Sometimes two friends get so tight with each other that they leave everyone else out. They are together constantly: they spend the night at each other's homes, wear each other's clothes, develop secret-coded languages, and are so close you would swear they have become Siamese twins.

This is not always healthy for a friendship. The reason? Sooner or later you will burn the relationship out. It's kind of like this: Remember the time you went on a food binge? Perhaps it was a craving for Fudgsicles. You ate those frozen delights whenever you could. You bought them by the box. People thought you were born with a wooden stick in your mouth. Then suddenly you changed. You overdosed on Fudgsicles. You no longer wanted them. They became unappealing, and you began to crave some other goody.

This happens with people, too. If you want your friendships to last, don't make them so binding that you leave no room for anyone else!

Be Able to Apologize

Even in friendships, problems can develop. Misunderstandings come up or one of you does something stupid. These become turning points in the friendship: The friendship can continue or bust apart. Usually what happens depends on the willingness of one or both friends to admit mistakes and apologize. Saying, "I'm sorry" costs nothing, except for a bit of pride.

Be Kind

Put-downs can be fun. Friends often joke around and put each other down in fun, but never with any seriousness. Yet sometimes put-down sessions turn bloody. Jokes are still jokes, but we no longer laugh. The jabs that used to be arrows with rubber suction cups on the ends are now barbed steel—intentional and well-aimed.

Because of this fact, people will often tell you that it's wrong to play with put-downs at all. I'm not going to tell you that, but it is important to learn when to stop teasing and what kind of put-downs should be avoided.

The most hurtful put-downs are those that poke fun at things we can't change. Talking like Porky Pig to a kid who stutters is not funny; it's *mean*. Trying to poke at somebody with our put-downs is not funny. It's cruel, and is a sign that we are not true friends.

Be Honest

The Bible contains an interesting quote: "Wounds from a friend are better than kisses from an enemy" (Proverbs 27:6 LB). True friends sometimes have to say things that are unpleasant in order to help us out. If you make a total fool out of yourself at the lunch table, a real friend will tell you. The truth may hurt, but at least it's the truth.

Forever Friends

It doesn't matter how many great friends you have or how popular you become, sooner or later you will need a friendship that is stronger than any a human being can offer you. You will need the friendship of the one who created you.

God is very interested in being your friend. But be warned: Dealing with God is not like messing around with school friends. He is very powerful and insists that people keep their bargains. And he has to be approached with a great deal of respect.

The great Christian writer C. S. Lewis created a series of children's stories in which Christ was portrayed as a powerful lion.[3] I have always thought that this was a very good image of God. Imagine that an intelligent but ferocious lion wanted to be friends with you. You wouldn't treat him like you do your pussy cat. You would approach him carefully and not tease him by pulling his whiskers. God wants to be your friend, but not in a casual, flippant manner. Remember, he is the King and Creator of the universe.

As you have learned from your human friendships, real

friendships are two-sided. If a person wants to be friends with another person who would prefer *not* to be friends, someone will be hurt. God wants to be your friend, but he will not force his friendship on you. You must want the friendship, too.

But saying that you want

God to be your friend and meaning it are two different things. A desire to be God's friend must be demonstrated. God has already gone a long way to prove that he wants to be your friend. Jesus once taught his disciples the greatest test of friendship that can be demonstrated. He said, "Greater love has no one than this, that he lay down his life for his friends" (John 15:13).

This is just what God did for you and me. He came to earth in human form and allowed himself to be crucified, so that he could take the punishment for the wrong things we have done. In other words, God changed places with you and me. He made the first gesture of friendship by dying on that dirt hill outside Jerusalem.

Like any other friendship, a friendship with God is one that cannot simply be accepted; it must be returned. God has offered his friendship and we must say to him in our hearts, "Yes, I want to be friends, too."

A friendship with God does have some similarities to your friendship with other kids. Consider the following ones:

The need to communicate. What kind of friendship would you have if you never spoke to your friend? A lousy one at best. God wants to hear from you. You can tell him anything, no matter how silly or insignificant. He likes to hear about the details of your life as well as the heavy stuff.

Some people make the mistake of thinking that they only need to talk to God when they have problems or a bucket of sins to dump at his door for forgiveness. Nah! God loves to hear about the things that interest you. After all, how would you like it if you had a friend who only spoke to you when she had a problem she wanted to be bailed out of? You would start to feel like a big fire escape, wouldn't you?

The act of talking to God is called *prayer*. And guess what? You can pray at any time. You don't even need to shut your eyes, fold your hands, or get on your knees. You can talk silently to God—he can hear your thoughts—or you can bellow to him out loud. You can pray as you walk to class; you can pray on the bus. Anywhere, any time, about anything.

And God wants to talk to you. Only rarely in history has God spoken in a voice that everyone could hear. He speaks through other people, circumstances, and his creation. Most often, he speaks through the Bible. It is the Word of God.

For some people, reading the Bible seems like a hassle.

But think of it this way: Suppose that a friend of yours writes you a note. What will you do when you receive it? Will you sit on it? Throw it away unread? Will you save it until Christmas? No way! You'll tear into that letter and read it as soon as you can.

Well, the best friend that you'll ever have has written you a note. It contains some very personal stuff about your life. If you take the time to read it, you'll grow to appreciate your friendship with God even more.

One word of caution: This note is a very long one, so don't try to read it all at once. Read it a little bit at a time. You'll be amazed at how God speaks to you.

The need for faithfulness. We damage our friendship with God when we ignore him or put other things before him. In a human friendship, if you run out on your friends every time something a little more interesting comes along, your friendship will not last long. If you are too busy or involved with other things to pay any attention to your friends, you'll find they evaporate.

God will not evaporate. But did you know that you can hurt his feelings? Check out Ephesians 4:30. Be very careful not to do anything that might harm your friendship with God.

The need to share your friend. A special friendship with God is something to be shared with others. God is big enough to give everyone who wants to be his friend special attention. Tell other people by your words and actions about your relationship to your creator.

One Final, Final Word

This special friendship with God is one that will outlast any of the human friendships that you make. Even your very best of friends will disappoint you from time to time.

They won't come through when you really need them to. But God will never ever fail you. Even though you may not always be able to understand what he is doing and why he is doing it, rest assured that he loves you and wants what's best for you, not only as you enter middle school, but as you live the rest of your life!

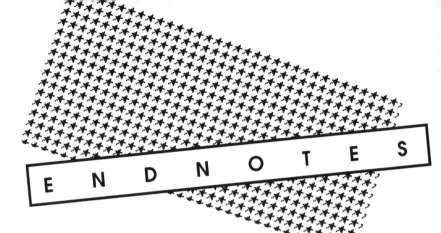

1. G. K. Chesterton, *Charles Dickens: A Critical Study* (London: Dodd Mead and Co., 1906), 8.

2. Quoting Wayne Rice, "Understanding Your Teenager" (Kauai, Hawaii, May 1990). This experiment is described in James Dobson, *Preparing for Adolescence* (Santa Ana, Calif.: Vision House, 1978), 47-48.

3. C. S. Lewis, *The Chronicles of Narnia* (New York: Macmillan Co., 1950).